Wife

Samuel Adamson's plays and adaptations include: *The Light Princess, Southwark Fair, Mrs Affleck, Frank & Ferdinand, Pillars of the Community* (National Theatre); *Running Wild* (Chichester Festival Theatre/Regent's Park Open Air Theatre); *Gabriel* (Globe); *Fish and Company* (Soho Theatre/National Youth Theatre); *Clocks and Whistles* (Bush Theatre); *Drink, Dance, Laugh and Lie* (Bush/Channel 4); *Grace Note* (Peter Hall Company/Old Vic); *Some Kind of Bliss* (Trafalgar Studios); *Tomorrow Week* (BBC Radio 3); *All About My Mother* (Old Vic); as well as original contributions to: *Hoard Festival* (New Vic, Stoke); *24 Hour Plays* (Old Vic); *A Chain Play* (Almeida); *Urban Scrawl* (Theatre 503); and *Decade* (Headlong). Versions include: *A Doll's House* (Southwark Playhouse); *Uncle Vanya* (West Yorkshire Playhouse); *The Cherry Orchard, Three Sisters* (Oxford Stage Company); *Professor Bernhardi, Larisa and the Merchants* (Arcola) and *Transdanubia Dreaming* (NT Studio).

T0322541

SAMUEL ADAMSON

Wife

FABER & FABER

First published in 2019
by Faber and Faber Limited
The Bindery, 51 Hatton Garden,
London EC1N 8HN

Typeset by Country Setting, Kingsdown, Kent CT14 8ES
Printed in England by CPI Group (UK) Ltd, Croydon CR0 4YY

A CIP record for this book
is available from the British Library

ISBN 978-0-571-35482-5

For Scott Forbes

1961–2018

Acknowledgements

I'm grateful to Julie Holledge, Professor at the Centre
for Ibsen Studies at the University of Oslo, for allowing
me to read, prior to publication, *A Global Doll's House:
Ibsen and Distant Visions* (Palgrave Macmillan, 2016)
by Julie Holledge, Jonathan Bollen, Frode Helland
and Joanne Tompkins. I was inspired by the authors'
investigations into the international reach of *A Doll's
House*, and the iconography of the tarantella and
tambourine; and by their notion of an 'identity space' for
actresses who have played Nora.

Thanks also to Indhu Rubasingham, Richard Porter,
Katie Haines, Scott Forbes, Nic Wass, Jennifer Bakst,
the actors who participated in readings, Richard Cant,
Karen Fishwick, Pamela Hardman, Joshua James,
Calam Lynch, Sirine Saba, and everyone at Kiln Theatre.

English text from *A Doll's House* was written with
reference to a literal translation by Charlotte Barslund,
from which I made my own version for a production
at Southwark Playhouse, London, in 2003.

Wife was first presented at the Kiln Theatre, Kilburn, on 30 May 2019. The cast, in alphabetical order, was as follows:

Peter / Landlord / Ivar at 58 Richard Cant
Daisy / Clare Karen Fishwick
Character Actress / Embassy Assistant / Marjorie
    Pamela Hardman
Robert / Ivar at 28 / Finn Joshua James
Eric / Cas Calam Lynch
Suzannah Sirine Saba

Director Indhu Rubasingham
Designer Richard Kent
Lighting Designer Guy Hoare
Sound Designer Alexander Caplen
Composer David Shrubsole
Movement Director Diane Alison-Mitchell
Assistant Director Breman Rajkumar
Casting Director Sarah Bird
Voice Coach Danièle Lydon

This play is written for six actors (three women and three men), with the following doubling:

Peter / Landlord / Ivar at 58
Character Actress / Embassy Assistant / Marjorie
Daisy also plays Clare
Robert / Ivar at 28 / Finn
Eric also plays Cas
Suzannah

Characters

Suzannah
Peter
Character Actress
Daisy
Robert
Ivar at 28
Eric
Embassy Assistant
Landlord
Cas
Director
(*voice only*)
Clare
Finn
Ivar at 58
Marjorie

WIFE

Why on earth didn't he just say straight out
to the Major 'No thank you very much – but
I'm not like that –' well perhaps not thank you
very much, but whatever it is in a case like that
you do say – and then just have gone on his way
like the others instead of hanging around
in the rain and complaining. The others
didn't complain, after all.

Terence Rattigan, *Separate Tables*
(alternative version)

. . . and it was so extraordinarily moving and
exciting when that spurt of recognition came,
like the flare of a match!

Alan Hollinghurst, *The Swimming Pool Library*

Act One

Projection

1959

Suzannah and Peter, 1879 costumes. A traditional, realistic staging of A Doll's House.

Suzannah Here's your ring. Give me mine. Do it.
    We're both free. I'll leave my keys here. Tomorrow Mrs Linde will come and pack my things, the things I owned before we were married. I'll have them sent on.

Peter It's over?
    Will you ever think of me?

Suzannah I will, often, and the children, and this house.

Peter At least let me send you some / money –

Suzannah I said no: I don't accept help from strangers.

Peter Will I ever be more than a stranger?

Suzannah For that we'd need something rare. The miracle.

Peter You keep speaking of a miracle, what miracle?

Suzannah The miracle that . . . we both change so completely that . . .
    I don't believe in the miracle any more.

Peter But I want to believe in it. Tell me. We both change so completely, that what?

Suzannah That together we share a life that's a true marriage.

15

Character Actress as Nursemaid enters, carrying and calming a crying baby.

Character Actress Mrs Helmer?

Suzannah Goodbye.

She leaves.

Peter Nora! Nora?
The miracle?

The street door slams.

Suzannah in her dressing room. Daisy and Robert, both twenties. Clipped, Rattiganesque.

Daisy It was at that garden party.

Suzannah With the politician. What was his name?

Daisy Enoch Powell.

Suzannah Yes.

Daisy A year ago.

Suzannah Yes.

Daisy I'd never have dared, but I thought, you only live once.

Suzannah Yes.

Daisy You don't mind?

Suzannah I let you up, didn't I?

Daisy You do remember?

Suzannah Your name's Mrs Elyot. Daisy.

Daisy Yes!

Suzannah A schoolmistress. You were reading a book by Elizabeth Taylor – not the actress, the novelist. You wore a lilac frock and a gardenia in your hair.

Daisy (*to Robert*) Told you. (*To Suzannah.*) He didn't believe I knew you.

Suzannah It's a Praetorian Guard at the door. Not just anybody gets through.

Daisy I spilled sherry on that frock.

Suzannah Hello.

She holds out her hand to Robert. He takes it unwillingly.

Daisy Robert You didn't meet that day. Don't know why.

Suzannah You'd just returned from your honeymoon, I think?

Daisy Yes.

Suzannah Singapore?

Daisy Windermere.

Suzannah Ah, the Lakes. 'I wander'd lonely as a cloud . . . something blah blah daffodils.'

Daisy What? Oh yes, Wordsworth. We saw his house. Did you make the film with Cary Grant?

Pause.

Suzannah What's your work, Mr Elyot?

Daisy Broker. Daddy's firm.

Pause.

Suzannah I think I have some gin somewhere –

Daisy Yes, we'd love a drink. Dutch courage.

But Suzannah doesn't move.

It's magical in here. Breathe it all in, Robert, soak it up.

Pause.

Suzannah Clearly, you hated it.

Daisy What?

Suzannah The play.

Daisy Oh. No! No no no, I loved it. It overwhelmed me. Its moral point-of-view was so touching and galvanizing and you: her – Nora – she was a force of nature –

Robert Moral point-of-view? You left your husband.

Suzannah Oh, it's alive. I am glad.

Robert Why?

Suzannah Glad it's alive?

Robert Why did you leave him?

Suzannah Nora? Well, as we say: if you have to ask.

Robert And what's so bloody magical about it? I've dumped in nicer rooms.

Daisy Robert.

Suzannah Yes, the theatre: it leaks, it stinks, it's full of unsinkable shits.

Pause.

Robert He was a good man. Secure job, bank manager, plenty of money, except when you were blowing it on brooches and hairbrushes. Perfect home with servants, children, everything you could want.

Daisy Exactly, not a real home, that's why it's called *A Doll's House*.

Suzannah Ibsen – (*Condescending to Robert.*) – the writer – is like a gunner. He shoots at everything conventional. Is it cotton if you've been married a year? Or paper?

18

Daisy I beg your pardon? Oh. Cotton, I think.

Suzannah Are you a housewife now, or . . . do you still teach?

Daisy I teach. Art. I love it. My pupils are so good.

Conversation dies.

I adore children –

Robert I'm not an idiot, I get it, something has to happen in a play, there has to be a secret –

Daisy Robert –

Robert – and yours was you broke the law.

Daisy Yes, but it was forgivable, you felt for Nora, because her husband had been sick, she needed money to pay for his treatment, that's the only reason she took the loan –

Robert Right, and forged her father's signature, because she wanted to help her husband, not buy more shoes and macaroons. And the loan shark came after you, and your husband found out, and you were *this* close to scandal. As he said: no religion, no morals. Then you got lucky. The loan shark found love, went soft and returned your IOU. And your husband forgave you. But what did you do? Decided that forgiveness was offensive and walked out on your marriage.

Suzannah Ta-da! All you need to know about *A Doll's House*: a woman walks.

Robert With nothing. Into nothing.

Suzannah Into everything, I think.

Robert This is why I hate the theatre.

Daisy We don't come very often. (*With programme.*) Will you sign, Miss Heywood?

Robert *My Fair Lady* was better. At least Julie Andrews sang a few songs.

Suzannah I'm pleased it's got under your skin.

Robert It's not under / my skin.

Suzannah The play still has it. Eighty years old and it's as sharp / as a pin.

Robert I'm just an ordinary bloke who calls out a lie when he sees one.

Suzannah One person's lie is another's / truth.

Robert Moral point-of-view? It was *im*moral. Act Four's missing.

Suzannah I beg your pardon?

Robert Ibsen – 'the writer' – where's his Act Four, when you come back?

Suzannah There are only three acts: thesis, antithesis, synthesis.

Robert Come on, you slammed that door, walked as far as Fortnum & Mason, calmed down over a nice cup of tea and a slice of Swiss / roll –

Daisy Robert –

Robert – then you crawled back to your master.

Suzannah I don't think they have Fortnum's in Norway.

Robert Just like the girl in *My Fair Lady*.

Suzannah But not the woman in *Pygmalion*.

Daisy I want you to know I thought you were magnificent –

Robert Yes, how *do* you remember all those words?

Suzannah I find I don't have anything to drink after all.

Daisy I'm so sorry –

Robert Why are you apologising?

Daisy This has all / gone wrong –

Robert She puts it out there, she tells her 'Praetorian Guard' to allow the crowd in, she has to know we're not all going to fall at her feet –

Suzannah Yes, an audience's response is its response.

Robert An 'audience' isn't one thing.

Suzannah You're even more obnoxious when you're right.

Robert It wasn't life.

Suzannah Just a reflection of it.

Robert It was unsinkable shit.

Suzannah Cock of the walk, aren't you?

Robert sweeps Suzannah's dressing table, violently. Props, make-up, etc. go flying.

Daisy My God.

Peter enters.

Peter Everything all right in here, old boy?

Suzannah Hello, darling. This is Mr and Mrs Elyot. Apparently at a garden party once I could have met Enoch Powell – you know, is he in the Cabinet? – but instead I met this lady. We chatted for a minute about the Lakes, Coniston Water and *Swallows and Amazons* and all that sort of thing, then tonight Giacomo rang up from the stage door and said, they're here.

Daisy You made such a good husband. I mean he was a ghastly husband but you were very good.

Robert We've a name for blokes like you in the City. 'Old Celery' – as in limp as.

Peter Good God, man, you're mistaking me for my role. You haven't understood the play at all.

Suzannah bursts out laughing. She kisses Peter passionately.

Suzannah Shall we go home?

Peter Home? Yes.

Suzannah Straight back to the flat.

Peter Whatever suits.

Suzannah No supper, all I want is bed.

Peter Jolly good.

Suzannah kisses him intensely again. Robert sniggers.

Robert Ta-da: Act Four. Wife crawls home to husband with his pipe and slippers.

Suzannah Except he's not my husband, he's the chum I fuck. I'd never marry him, nor anybody. I don't allow anyone to impose his morality on me or diminish me. I've slammed more doors on men than you've had hot dumps.

Daisy Dear God . . .

Robert Come on, Daisy. We'll miss our bus.

Peter Yes, I think you'd better trot off.

Daisy Gosh . . . gosh, I'm awfully sorry, Miss Heywood –

Suzannah Goodbye. Good luck.

Robert and Daisy leave.

Peter Well, I'm dashed. Heck of an invasion.

Suzannah My fault. Thank you, Peter.

Peter I've wanted to kiss you for four months.

Suzannah I'm glad it was you who walked in, not Harelip Marjorie from wigs. Good night.

Peter Right. Jolly good. Happy to serve. Night-night, old boy.

He retreats. Suzannah cleans up. After a time, Daisy returns. Suzannah takes no notice.

Daisy I'm so silly, I forgot my programme.
I just wanted to say . . .
He's waiting. Our bus.
I often think I earn enough in my job – for everything I need or would like, I mean. So we could take a cab, but he's anxious about money. He wants to prove himself to my father. Anyway, that's why he's always so . . .
I'm awfully, awfully . . .
Please.
Please.
Suzannah.

Suzannah has a prop – a tambourine. Daisy stops her from ignoring her, clutches her.

Suzannah You have to go.

Daisy He can wait.

Suzannah He won't wait long.

Daisy I'm drunk.

Suzannah Oh, is that it?

Daisy Like I always am when I'm with you or you come into my mind. My year of inebriation. Two days ago I was . . . at the doctor's and . . . I came out . . . and drunkenly I walked and walked all the way to the box office and handed over the money for the tickets. When I got home he was furious at the expense. Drunkenly, I didn't care. Drunkenly, I wanted him to see you.

Suzannah Let go.

Daisy Rub his nose in it.

Suzannah Snout.

Daisy Yes, to shove his snout in this, this . . . swill . . . this . . . delicious . . . *mess* . . . and tonight drunkenly I, I told him I knew you – that I'd met you just once – and on the pavement I found myself suggesting we say hello and then drunkenly here we were.

Suzannah I don't know what / to say –

Daisy And it felt so good! And the play, I didn't realise it had got to him, and my goodness how you skewered him! At the Tate, there's this painting by Waterhouse of the Lady of Shalott floating towards Sir Lancelot, wearing white, her eyes fatalistic, she's going to drown, there are candles in her boat, two have blown out, one's horizontal in the wind, it's all concocted to excite every single one of your neurons – and Robert? Nothing. I play Chopin extremely movingly on the piano, he tells me he's going to sell it, I read him Wordsworth – *in the Lakes* – he glazes over, yet tonight he was pricked –

Suzannah He was threatened. He knows what you like.

Daisy No one knows.

Suzannah To bring him here, Daisy, have you lost your mind?

Daisy kisses her. Suzannah resists, receives it, pushes her off.

Daisy Don't be angry with me, little squirrel.
    Nifty work with Peter, by the way. That kiss looked very real and serious.
    He loves you, you know.

Suzannah Yes.

Daisy (*laughs*) Poor sad Peter, poor old Pierrot – (*Stops.*) It's *not* serious, is it?

God, that glorious play! (*Takes tambourine.*) This was my favourite bit. When Nora danced the tarantella.

She flourishes it and dances provocatively, Nora-like, but this is incongruous with her clothes (and personality).
Suzannah grabs the tambourine and snaps.

Suzannah No one ever encouraged me to be an individual. Not my parents, nor my school – school! – full of nuns who were frauds, or terrified, and this suited most of the girls, but there were three of us who thought we were fighting back, the 'fighting' that comes from a secret, being in love, sex, because sex makes you feel powerful. I understand, it's what you felt when you watched me tonight with him sitting right next to you: the power of your secret, and you wanted to brandish it, kill with it, but the truth is, all you've done is pinch a blind man and run away. To have a secret feels like power, but it's nothing just to keep it, it's only powerful when it's out, really *out*. At school, I was a little pincher, and I changed nothing about that prison. One grows up and stops being so cowardly.

Daisy Oh yes, you're such a mature thing now, such a warrior.

Suzannah What do you mean by that?

Daisy Easy to be one here in the theatre – all safe from the world.

Suzannah Yes. Perhaps.

Daisy It's still your prison. It's just the walls are now velvet curtains and the nuns are fairies.

Suzannah (*chuckles*) Well, I know where I belong.

Daisy Lucky you. Obviously, you're still lonely.

Suzannah As lonely as you, Mrs Elyot?

Daisy Me? I'm not lonely, my husband and I have riveting conversations over our porridge every morning. Many subjects. The atomic bomb. The trouble with Princess Margaret. Who's at your breakfast table?

Suzannah That depends which chorus girl from *My Fair Lady* has stayed the night – and how many.

Daisy Oh, don't make it sound like you haven't paid a price to be you –

Suzannah Of course I have: everyone does if they're themselves! It's my life you've come into, Daisy, mine – the very fact you brought him here tonight to make a sport of me shows how much you relish it, so don't turn on it out of envy now.

Daisy I didn't want to make a sport of / you –

Suzannah What were you thinking?

Daisy And I'm not envious. Where's your sense / of fun?

Suzannah You're breaking the rules –

Daisy Rules!

Suzannah You of all people know / the rules –

Daisy So I'm right: you're not so free as you pretend, Madam Bohemia.

Suzannah Oh flit back to Chelsea, you blithering fool.

Daisy All right, you're right, I envy you!
    I just wanted to . . . get to him . . . bore a hole through him . . .

Suzannah Go, he'll know something's up by now. I feel like I have to disinfect / the –

Daisy Suzannah –

Suzannah I never posture, Daisy, so here it is: I never want to see that man again.

Daisy I'm pregnant.

Suzannah stares. She goes to the bathroom. Daisy goes straight to a place where a bottle of gin is kept, pours some into a teacup, drinks. More. She notices something on the tambourine. Feelings reined in, Suzannah returns, prepares to leave.

What are these names written on it?

Suzannah Just names.

She takes tambourine, busies herself.

Daisy I'll cherish your Nora. It's as if you spoke directly to me. She made me feel as if . . . one should always get oneself out of one's bind . . . because the world always holds promise. Somewhere.

Suzannah It's only a play. They change nothing. Whatever sprouted in you will be dead in a week.

Daisy What are you doing?

Suzannah What does it look like?

Daisy Can I come home with you?

Suzannah Jesus Christ, Daisy, Jesus / Christ.

Daisy Please don't – (*Chokes in agony.*)

Suzannah I assumed – no, you told me – you said that you and Robert didn't / have –

Daisy We don't. Not really . . .

Suzannah I don't understand.

Daisy I didn't have a choice. I mean I didn't try to stop him, but –

Suzannah Did you choose it or not?

Daisy No.

Suzannah He forced himself on you?

Daisy Well, he didn't exactly claim his conjugal rights or anything, but . . .

Suzannah But? But what?

Daisy It had been months since our last . . . fumble, and he kept going on about the firm and Daddy's expectations for our future and . . . one night he was just . . . on me . . . so I closed my eyes, / and –

Suzannah Sounds as if he claimed his so-called rights to me!

Daisy Suzannah –

Suzannah You know, you say no one knows about you, Daisy, but your family does, your father's on it like a bloodhound, it's why he gave Robert a job, that's why he invited Robert for dinner every Friday for a year till he proposed – that's the inevitable, horrific thing: your family is why you're married.

Daisy You make me sound as if I have no authority whatsoever –

Suzannah Do you? Did you want a wedding? Did you want him inside you?

Daisy Of course not. I want you. The whole time I thought of you, please help me, please / help –

Suzannah How can I / help!

Daisy I'll get rid of it.

Suzannah Daisy –

Daisy You know what to do, you being you, you must know of someone / or, or –

Suzannah Me being me? You do look down on me, don't you? Who am I, Nell from the playhouse? Cor blimey, ain't it exotic on the wrong side of the tracks? A gallon of gin and a hot bath, that'll do it, dearie. Oranges, oranges, tuppence for an / orange!

Daisy The truth is it's you who consistently condescends to me, you've done it since I walked in. You despise me because you think I'm nothing but a daughter and a wife.

I don't think you have any idea what you mean to me . . .

Our afternoons together are the loveliest things that have ever happened to me in my whole life.

I could have it . . . and we could still . . . or I could do something about it, and . . .

Help.

She clutches Suzannah. The phone rings. Suzannah is torn. The phone stops.

Suzannah We're going on tour. Paris to Warsaw, all the stops in between. Belgrade. Zagreb.

Daisy So I'll see you tomorrow?

The phone rings again. Suzannah groans, detaches herself from Daisy, answers it.

Suzannah Yes?
I'm sorry, Giacomo.
Fine. (*Hangs up.*)

Daisy Three-thirty as usual.

Suzannah He's on his way up –

Daisy It's Friday tomorrow, I only teach till noon on Fridays –

Suzannah I can't.

Daisy Yes you / can!

Suzannah Daisy, / I can't –

Daisy And I wonder, perhaps this week we might even step out, to the Tate / or –

Suzannah I want you to go –

Daisy After we've had our fun here of course – / on this enchanting floor –

Suzannah Don't you understand, I can't bear it, I can't *bear that that pig touches you.*

Daisy But you can't be jealous of him, that won't help anything, let's just fix it together –

Suzannah Go –

Daisy You're in my skin –

Suzannah Why, / why? –

Daisy Touch me.

Suzannah Why? –

Daisy I'll leave him.

Suzannah What?

Daisy I'll come with you on tour –

Suzannah laughs, disbelief.

I'll take Marjorie's job, what a bossy woman, and blinded by her infatuation: you were adorable tonight but your Act Two wig looked like the Bride of Frankenstein's –

Suzannah *Why have you ruined it?*

Daisy But I didn't: *I. Didn't.*

Her legs won't support her.

Suzannah This has happened to you.
  I care for you, / but –

30

Daisy No, don't say that, it's more than that . . .

Suzannah I can't be dominated by someone else. I have some power not to allow that, and I won't compromise it.

Daisy I love you –

Suzannah Please get up, leave –

Daisy Don't do this.

Suzannah He's coming.

Daisy Suzannah –

Suzannah Then I'll go, I have a car, I'll collect Peter and if I see your husband on the stairs I'll walk straight past him.

Daisy Please –

Suzannah What are you going to do, stay there all night?

Daisy Yes, for ever.

Silence.

Suzannah I can't live with his child. And I can't live with your loss of a child. Don't come back.

She leaves. Daisy is at a loss for some time. She picks up a pen. She can't find anything to write on. Only the tambourine. She writes – and draws – on that. Robert enters.

Robert Daisy?
What are you doing?

Daisy Suzannah's just gone to . . . gone to speak . . . to the . . . woman who does her hair. Marjorie. It's amusing: she does hair, and she has a harelip.

Robert Has she?

Daisy Yes, poor thing, it's quite pronounced.

Robert I meant has 'Suzannah' gone?
'Suzannah'? Not Miss Heywood?
Why did we come here?

Daisy I can't catch a bus. For once you're going to have to dig into your shopkeeper pockets and find the money for a (*cab*) –

She chokes, cries, tries to stop, can't.

Robert This isn't how it's going to be.

Daisy Going to be?

Robert Why did you bring me here?

Daisy To see a play, it does one good to see a play, especially one that provokes one.

Robert Don't treat me like a fool.

Daisy Then don't act like one.

She is a wreck, makes no attempt to hide it.

Robert I can't do that . . . I won't . . . before we were married . . . your father said / you –

Daisy Oh, what did Daddy say?

Robert He / said –

Daisy I'd wager Daddy's slept with more actresses than you've had 'hot dumps', so to hell with / Daddy –

Robert He used a word, 'invert', I didn't know / what it meant –

Daisy (*laughs*) 'Invert', what a ridiculous / man!

Robert 'Marjorie, who does her hair, *Suzannah's hair*'? – *Get up.*

Daisy Don't shout.

Robert How many times have you come here? Who's seen you?

Daisy People have, I suppose.

Robert People we know?

Daisy I crashed into your sweet Cockney aunt on Drury Lane one / afternoon –

Robert Stop it.

Daisy – and you were blind if you didn't notice the smirk on the stage-door man's face when he let us in – Giacomo's seen it all, it's Oscar Wilde to him.

Robert Stop it, if you were a man you'd get five years for this –

Daisy Lucky I'm a woman! –

Robert Christ. Dear God. You don't think you're *her*, do you?

Daisy Who?

Robert That caveman. Tell me you don't think that?

Daisy I don't understand.

Robert In the fucking play. Nora, that ape. Only an ape wouldn't understand. No one found out she forged the signature – because he covered it up for her! Only a child or a caveman couldn't see that *that* was her precious 'miracle'. Their secret stayed secret. He shut the lid. No shame, no need for her to walk.

She left her own children. What kind of woman . . . what sort of mother does that?

A moment. Daisy punches her stomach.

Oh no . . . no no no . . . stop it . . .

Daisy pushes him off, they struggle, entwined, on to the floor.

33

Are you pregnant? . . . stop it, stop it . . . *it's not the done thing.*

It stops. Silence.

Have I understood? Daisy? Have I?

Pause. Daisy nods tightly.

Have you understood me?

Daisy Perfectly.

She stands, repairs herself – becomes, in a few swift moves, impeccably 1950s.

I have work in the morning.

Robert Have you told your father?

Daisy Told him what?

Robert About this, Daisy!

Daisy No.

Robert We must ring him up straight away. The school?

Daisy What about it?

Robert Have you told the headmistress?

Daisy There's plenty of time.

Robert You'll do it tomorrow.

Daisy I'm not due for months.

Robert I said you'll inform the school tomorrow, you hear? It's only reasonable.

Daisy How so?

Robert They'll need to find someone to replace you.

Daisy turns to him on this, stares.

It's intolerable you kept working after we married in the first place. You're my wife.

34

Daisy (*at length, doesn't take her eyes off him*) For the avoidance of doubt, I saw Suzannah. Many times. I noticed her at the garden party and dared to talk to her. She touched my face and said she didn't care Daddy was watching and she asked me to tea – 'tea or something stronger', those were her words. So I came, I came again, everything your imagination is telling you happened, happened. It's over, and I assure you the done thing is the one thing I'll always do, but you must promise never to refer to it again. You must promise.

She holds out her hand. He takes it. A sad, perfunctory shake.

Well, hurry up, darling, we'll miss the bus.

Robert Right.

Daisy Tuck your shirt in.

They stare. She leads him out. A moment. She returns and collects the tambourine. She wants more than anything to put it back, but doesn't. The machinery of Wife *is exposed: Stage Managers enter. A mellifluous female voice on a loop recording is heard. Daisy is lost to the transition.*

Recorded Voice To opt out of live simultaneous translation, press stop, remove earphones and return them to the back of the seat in front of you. To adjust volume, press plus or minus. To opt out of live simultaneous translation, press . . .

Etc. An electronic soundscape as Suzannah and Peter enter in a shaft of light, in a violent and bloody struggle, the power his. A symbolist, avant-garde staging.

Suzannah La meg gå! La meg gå, la meg gå!

Peter Er det sant hva han skriver, Nora? En hyklerske, en løgnerske – en forbryterske?

Suzannah Jeg har elsket deg over alt i verdens rike.

Peter Fy, fy! Ingen religion, ingen moral. Du blir altså fremdeles her i huset. Men børnene får du ikke lov til å oppdra. Forstår du nu hva du har gjort imot meg, Nora? Nora? Nora?

> *Climactically, Suzannah faces him, calm and cold, and gains the power. Character Actress enters as Nursemaid carrying and calming a crying baby. Unlike Suzannah and Peter's modernist costumes, hers is 1879 traditional, identical to the opening; and her moves are exactly the same.*

Character Actress Fru Helmer?

Projection

1988

Suzannah Ja. Now I am beginning to understand everything. Ja.

> *The street door slams.*

Act Two

Ivar, late-twenties, and Eric, twenty, tightly lit – a corner table, a busy pub. Ivar has just got drinks. Eric drinks quickly. They enter into a private game in a public space: their smut is secret, though Ivar becomes erratically, dangerously flagrant. They never touch.

Ivar (*toasts*) Cum in your eye.

Eric Cheers.

Ivar You get what I'm saying, Eric? It got to the heart of *us*, it was *our lives* – did it make you hard?

Eric I've had a stiffy all night, Lady Diana.

Ivar A 'stiffy', bless. Fuck me.

Eric In here?

Ivar Bone me in this heterosexual jungle.

Eric If you think you can take it, Lady Di.

Ivar Plough me in the name of Ibsen.

Eric Gob on it first.

Ivar Manners.

Eric Piss on it, slag.

Ivar Easy, tiger.

Eric Open wide, I'm going to knob you till you detonate –

Ivar Without a condom, what will society say!

Eric Screw them, screw them, screw them – (*Grunts, active.*)

Ivar (*groans, passive*) And that's the point. It was on the front line, ahead of its time, it's like a, a priceless cave painting, a marker in history so we can say, 'Look how far we've come' –

 Eric grunts.

(*Groans.*) Because you and I, Eric – harder harder, Eric – *we have what the wife wanted.*

Eric Yes.

Ivar Her feminist call – no, her humanist ejaculation – was heard.

Eric Yes.

Ivar Our relationship is proof.

Eric Oh, yes.

Ivar This –

Eric Good –

Ivar – feels –

Eric – Daddy –

Ivar – so –

Eric – nice –

Ivar – galvanising –

Eric – hole –

Ivar – whole, we are one whole.

Eric Take –

 Ivar squeals.

– that.

Ivar We have this sink – sink – sink it in, boy –

Eric Don't let me come –

Ivar – synchronicity.

Eric Eat my bronze eye, Lady Di –

Ivar slurps.

– deeper,

Ivar slurps.

deeper –

Ivar And no one in this horrifying pub has a clue! They don't even realise –

Eric That right now you're tonguing my / moist –

Ivar – our deeply personal bond. Completely self-determining, utterly separate from the Heterosexual Empire.

Eric Heterosexual / Empire!?

Ivar The fundamentalist Federation of Breeders i.e. –

Points around – the rest of the pub is often Wife's *audience.*

– them. Look at that stag party over there, what a smug cluster of milk-snatching Maggiemaggots –

Eric laughs.

– I'm serious. (*Towards stag party; risky.*) Wankers! (*To Eric.*) Take me up the fjord.

Eric I just wanted to go and see *A Fish Called Wanda* tonight.

Ivar It wouldn't have had the same impact.

Eric I mean, it was a *play* –

Ivar It was a mirror –

Eric In Norwegian, bitch.

Ivar *Ja* – first time I've heard you say bitch, Alexis /
Colby –

Eric It was an ancient foreign play, we had to wear
earphones – I must fancy / you –

Ivar *Ja ja*, check it out, Norway 1879, *ja / ja ja* –

Eric (*'Norwegian' via Roald Dahl*) Oompa loompa
doompedy / doo –

Ivar But you loved it?

Eric (*via* Mork & Mindy) Nanu Nanu, / Nora –

Ivar And you *got* it?

   Eric grunts, grunts.

Harder, as if our lives depended on it, / Eric –

Eric I'm at it like the Duracell bunny, Diana, sometimes
it's like I want to be inside you because I want to *be* you /
you know?

Ivar You *are* me –

Eric Actually share the same skin –

Ivar That's what we're saying: we *do*. Nothing's dividing
us and there are no secrets between us –

Eric None –

Ivar – and do I dominate you, or you me? – No! Are
you, or I, the doll of some coke-snorting Filofax-
worshipping stockbroker tosser boy-racing home from
Morgan Stanley in his Lamborghini spunking all over his
Dire Straits CDs? – No! (*Towards stag party; louder,
riskier.*) Yuppie plankton! (*To Eric.*) Screw marriage,
screw the conformity and tyranny of it – because what
you and I have is a *private* love –

Eric Yes yes, I love that I met / you, yes –

Ivar – founded on shared attitudes and respect and mutual desire and equality – in our own community – our unique and self-sustaining undercover sisterhood of, um um um, fabulously ungodly nuns, in our homo habits –

Eric Nights like this, you make me / feel . . . (*Searches for word.*)

Ivar – and whatever I have access to, so do / you –

Eric – safe, I'm flying and it's / safe.

Ivar Everything's equally-ours because it's *only ours*: where did we meet? – Our own Greek planet. What do we share? – Our own culture, history, economy, sphincters; tonight reminded us nothing's stopping us from living the life we want –

Eric We're free.

Ivar (*à la Mr Humphries from* Are You Being Served?, *towards stag party, even louder.*) I'm free!

Eric (*flinches*) Shhh, not too / loud –

Ivar As if *they* understand, they can't speak Polari!

Eric What's Polari?

Ivar (*gasps, pearl-clutchingly 1950s*) I sold the family heirlooms so you could read Lavender Studies at Cupcake Polytechnic and *this* is how you repay me?

Eric Vada the lallies on her.

Ivar Oooh, who – the Hooray Henry? Bona, darling, dangerous – how much do we love Kirsty MacColl? –

He erupts into Billy Bragg/Kirsty MacColl's 'A New England'. Eric joins in, they both feel it, but Eric soon continues the game.

Eric Bang.

Ivar Poor miserable straight people. (*Grunts.*)

Eric Bang. Me.

Ivar Enslaved by normality. (*Grunts.*)

Eric Bang. Me. Like.

Ivar We simply don't recognise – (*Grunts.*)

Eric Bang me like a –

Ivar Your vanilla authority. (*Grunts.*)

Eric Bang me like a big –

Ivar Church of England. (*Grunts.*)

Eric Bang me like a big bloody –

Ivar Thatcher government. (*Big grunt.*)

Eric (*big groan*) Thank you, Lady Diana –

Ivar Thank you, *Nora*. (*Grunts.*)

Eric (*groans*) Bloody Nora.

Ivar Thank you.

Eric Bloody –

Ivar Tits, I forgot to set the VCR for *Neighbours*.

Eric (*groans*) Bloody –

Ivar (*grunts, sees someone, off*) Bloody hell –

Eric Don't stop –

Ivar – it's bloody –

Eric Bloody Nora.

Ivar – Nora.

Eric Shag my mothershagging –

Ivar Jesus wept, it's *actually* Nora.

Eric – clunge.

Ivar Eric, look: it's her: *Nora*.

At last, a pause. Ivar points excitedly. Eric looks. Unthinkingly, Ivar reaches to touch him. Eric pulls back to avoid his hand.

Oops. I know. (*Slaps wrist.*) Don't break the rules.

Pub noise. Eric glances towards the stag party self-consciously.

Who are those monstrous-looking trolls with her? We have to go and introduce ourselves.

Eric What?

Ivar We have to tell her.

Eric Tell her what?

Ivar About this, us, everything. (*Waves flamboyantly, can't stop staring.*)

Eric No. No . . . let's just . . . let's go back to yours and fuck on your futon.

Ivar You mean fuck for *real*? – How novel.

Eric (*stares, pauses*) I've got work tomorrow.

Ivar What? Work?

Eric Daisy needs me first thing.

Ivar Daisy?

Eric Yeah.

Ivar 'Daisy needs me first thing'?

Eric It's all right for you, you can open your gallery any time you like.

Ivar No, I can't –

Eric She wants me to move some furniture in her lounge. Or you could do my shift?

Ivar No, that's why I let my penis do the hiring and gave the job to you.

Eric Yeah, we're so 'equal', Ivar, with you my boss.

Ivar You could be mine.

Eric What, if my mum needed looking after? You'd clean her –? (*Mouths/indicates 'piss'.*)

Ivar Yes, I'd happily be her carer – it's *my* horrible incontinent gin-soaked mother I can't stand, I'd be delighted to wipe the fanny of *yours*, I'm desperate to meet her! (*Re. Nora.*) Come on!

Eric Why do you say stuff like that about your mum?

Ivar Because it's true.

Eric I like her. She's funny.

Ivar Drunks often are. So are homophobes. Mrs Elyot, double the fun.

Eric You washed your hands of her but you pay me to do things for her, so I have to respect her –

Ivar See this is why I love you so much: you're paradoxically filthy *and* pure, a sort of buggering Bambi.

Eric I promised I'd move her sofa –

Ivar Fuck's sake! –

Eric She's getting a piano, she wants to play again –

Ivar Piano? My mother's never played the piano!

Eric No? She said . . . Chopin or something? –

Ivar No! See? It's always a trap. A very well-bred trap. She's called Daisy, in fact she's Deadly Nightshade: Do Not Pluck. (*Re. Nora.*) Oh my God, she smokes like Katharine Hepburn.

Eric Who?

Ivar Darling! You're like a novice from *The Sound of Music*. *The Philadelphia Story*!

Eric Haven't the foggiest.

Ivar Then I shall lift the fog.

Tops up Eric's glass from his own.

Dutch courage.

Eric (*small chuckle of recognition*) 'Dutch courage.' Your mum says that.

Ivar (*toasts*) Yeah, up Daisy's – (*Stops.*) Christ, you don't drink with her, do you?

Eric No. She offers.

Ivar Oh, she's always impeccably polite. Then you look into her cold, scathing eyes and realise she's having a wazz on the carpet.

Eric Ivar. I don't want a hangover –

Ivar You're a baby fruit, baby fruits don't / get hangovers –

Eric Don't call me a / fruit –

Ivar Oh, Eric, honey, Nora's right there! This is like . . . that night we watched *My Beautiful Laundrette*. You'd never seen yourself in a film before and there you were –

Eric Keep going, Lady Di, let's see how far you can look down your nose –

45

Ivar – there *we* were, men fucking, no men in love, our lives actually in front of us for once. Daniel Day-Lewis just walked in. With Elton John. And Elton's female wife Renate.

Swaggering roars from the stag party. Eric looks.

Eric You're gonna get all . . . girlie, / and –

Ivar Girlie?

Eric You know what I . . . Stag mob, they keep looking.

Ivar If you're so worried perhaps you should take your willy out of my bottom.

Eric 'Bottom', you posh git – and yours is still up mine.

Ivar It's so cavernous in there I can't always tell.

Eric Pass me a spoon when I do you, it's like humping Christmas trifle.

Ivar (*very loud*) *Douze points* to the gay!

Eric (*cowers*) Ivar –

Ivar Devon knows how she makes it so creamy!

Eric Maybe I'll scream you're a nonce.

Ivar Ooooh, up to eleven, I like it –

Eric Still five whole months till I'm twenty-one –

Ivar Are you going to grass on me? *Do*: I'd go to Reading Gaol for you. While I'm having some of Her Majesty's pleasure you can stay out here bonking women. (*Re. pub.*) Isn't it astounding that by their standards you've been legal for five whole years? I feel we can now play Level Twelve: Fisting. (*Forms fist.*) Say hello to Mrs T, (*Mimics Thatcher.*) 'I love to stick it up the campers and I *never* use Vaseline' –

He punches at Eric, Eric dodges him.

Eric Jesus, stop it, not in here – that's not how it goes, stop being so camp.

Ivar stares at him. Pause. Suddenly, in mock terror of the stag party, he screams.

Ivar Sorry, I've got the Girlie Virus, there's no cure.

Eric We're out of here –

Ivar Only if we can shag at your place, *please* let me come and meet your parents – the only way to get rid of a temptation is to yield to / it –

Eric *Game over.*

Silence.

Ivar Lucky you're so pretty or I'd never condone it. Seriously. I wouldn't.

Eric I love you, Ivar . . . It's just . . . please . . . let's go now.

Ivar is surprised and moved by the declaration, however qualified. He mouths 'You love me!' like a silent film actress. He pantomimes casting a fishing rod and reeling it in to confirm the catch. No bite . . . then Eric is 'hooked' in the cheek, he's a whopper, silliness and smiles all round. Ivar makes to touch Eric again, but he pulls back.

Ivar Yeah. Right. We're off.

Slams down glass and heads off, only to turn on his heel and glide the other way.

Eric Ivar . . . no, Ivar!

Ivar has gone, Eric is on his own. He wants to leave. A rowdy song from the stag party. He is very uncomfortable. Ivar returns with Suzannah, chatting ad lib.

Ivar Detailed . . . and heart-stopping . . . and deeply relevant to both of us – Eric, Suzannah Leonardsen; Suzannah Leonardsen, Eric Hurst my wife, when I say wife I don't mean in the Anglican mode, I could just as easily have called him my hudson, as in Rock, we need a radical new word, something Italian, like *innamorato*, except not gender-specific . . . he's my, um, swain, and I'm his.

Suzannah Hello.

Eric Hi.

Ivar See, you didn't catch Aids by meeting her. (*To Suzannah.*) He reads the *Sun* so it *is* possible he thinks you can get it from toilet seats and Norwegians.

Eric (*speechless at this for a long moment*) You were . . . really good.

Ivar A simple way of putting it but correct, you were really good, really –

Suzannah I know, I'm outstanding in it, I know that.

Ivar Really, you've defined our lives – because, you see, Eric and I are what Nora demanded from her husband. A true marriage, not of laws, vicars, grim honeymoons in Windermere, years of gin-fuelled misery, but a marriage of minds and souls. What we saw tonight was *our story*, Nora slammed the door on a broken, obsolete system for *us*, and now a hundred years later we have this free, independent union that's not answerable to the interventions of the state and thrives irrespective of it.

Suzannah (*pauses*) Usually people just want me to sign their programmes.

Ivar We want to tattoo your name on our perinea – see Patriarchy Stag Party over there in Section 28? From the view of the fairies at the bottom of the garden – us – *they* are society's deviants, they are . . . a degenerate heavy metal band called . . . The Deficiency Syndrome, disgusting infected freaks, and we fly high above them, in a, well for want of a word, utopia that has none of their hypocritical rules and / rituals –

Eric Ivar –

Ivar – Let that banker have his traditional wedding and inevitable affairs and divorce, because here's the crux: for us there's no need for marriage so there's no need for divorce – Get me a knife, because I'm going to cut my wrist and mix my blood with Eric's right now: *we are Nora's miracle.*

He grabs Eric's face – their first physical contact in the scene – and kisses him forcefully. The pub falls silent. For now Suzannah fails to notice Eric's mortification.

Suzannah Do you have any cocaine?

Ivar Um. No.

Suzannah I think you've just made sense of my life. (*Indicates.*) My companions, from the Norwegian Embassy, Ibsen's pillars of society, they think a pub is the nearest thing to an actress's natural habitat, so here we are – in The Frog and Trumpet. Some drugs would help – my septum's necrotized, see? – My daughter loves it too, I had her out of wedlock when that was – (*Noise: taboo.*) I'm on my fourth husband – and what you just said? I've just realised: I'm not punished for any of it! The Ambassador just told me that because I'm playing Nora round the world, he could pull strings and help me with my tax arrears – I owe *lots of tax*. Yes, it's *my* miracle: I can do as I like because of the theatre, because of Nora! I'd love to test the theory by snorting a line off your bum in front of them. Well. Goodbye.

Ivar (*laughs*) You can't go now. My bum is yours. Have a drink.

Suzannah Kind, but it doesn't have the necessary hit and I have no idea who you are.

Ivar My name is Lady Diana Spencer, and my gay protégé and I always acknowledge our influences and forebears, so to thank you for being a Norwegian who played the Norwegian who paved our world, I insist on buying you a tequila.

He leaves. Suzannah laughs. But Eric is very agitated, a coiled spring.

Suzannah Lady Diana. Lucky Charles.

Eric (*snaps*) I'm not with him, we're not together.

Suzannah Oh? (*Looks in direction of Ivar. Back to Eric.*) Oh.
How old are you?
Younger than him.
How did you meet?

Eric In the mud. The bloody mud, we met in the mud.

Embassy Assistant enters, carrying a briefcase. Her moves replicate Character Actress.

Embassy Assistant Fru Leonardsen?

Suzannah waves her away, reasonably politely, and she exits. Suzannah rolls a cigarette.

Suzannah *Et dukkehjem* – A dollhome – that's the correct translation – is based on a true story. The real wife stayed. That wouldn't make a play, but it's life. Oh, Ibsen was right, there was a double standard – women don't stay with cruel, conventional men now if they don't want – but the truth is we have to give up parts of ourselves if we want to be with someone. And what if, before you know this, you let the right person go? What if you're with an idealist – a Nora, a sparking firebrand?

(*Looks in direction of Ivar.*) Unfortunately the world is always miles behind our Noras. We're very lucky if we get to meet them. We must cherish them. They give us hope. (*Lights up, shrugs.*) Well, life's messy.

Eric His mother and me got pissed on a gallon of gin and snogged and very nearly fucked, so that's pretty messy.

Pause.

Suzannah *Ja.* And as if I'm not going to have to pay the motherfucking tax.

Ivar returns with three shots of tequila.

Ivar Your stimulants, Miss Leonardsen. They're out of cocaine.

Suzannah Actors can't be choosers.

Ivar To you and Nora – goddesses.

Suzannah No, don't deify women like that, it takes away our complexities and contradictions. I'm not a fag hag. To you – and to Eric. *Skål.*

Ivar *Skål.*

They toast and drink, Eric doesn't toast but drinks. Embassy Assistant returns.

Suzannah Goodbye. (*Puts her hand on Eric's.*) Goodbye.

Her exit is identical to Nora's in the opening. Embassy Assistant follows. Ivar watches. He looks at Eric. The stag party plays a drinking game. Silence between them.

Ivar I want you to move in with me.

Silence: Eric could explode but daren't. Landlord comes to their table.

Landlord Closing time.

Ivar What?

Landlord You heard.

Ivar No it's not, there's half an hour.

Landlord Let's not make an issue of it.

Ivar Um . . . for what reason?

Landlord I don't need a reason. (*To Eric, re. his still half-full glass.*) Finished?

Eric nods tightly, cold with fear.

If I'd seen it, I'd have asked Tessa not to serve you, all right?

He reaches for Eric's glass, Ivar gets there first, they touch, Landlord reacts.

Ivar Oooh, did we just touch?

Eric Ivar –

Ivar I was chopping a cucumber at lunch and I nicked my finger. There was blood all over me, b.l.o.o. / d. –

Eric Ivar –

Ivar – so I know when I come to write a letter to the brewery, which are you, the Frog or the Trumpet? (*Sips defiantly.*)

Landlord This is my patch and you need to shift your shirtlifting arses.

Ivar Oh, your 'patch'? No: your patch is the whole country – Downing Street, Lewisham, Tunbridge Wells – our patch is, presently, this table, I'm not asking for more than this, but *I am insisting on this* –

Eric (*erupts; re. Ivar*) Queer. Faggot.

Landlord Drink up and get out, ladies.

He leaves.

Ivar Don't move. I'm not joking.

Silence.

I'll take queer. I am. And bent, I like bent. Shirtlifter and faggot, bit of an issue, possibly 'invert' gets to me – well, it would, if you walk past the kitchen and overhear your grandfather and father using this curious word, they were obviously talking about me, I was what? Twelve, but the difference between 1972 and 1988 is I can't stay silent. What did I do, rape you? Or, or I get it, this is the bit after the sex where you hate yourself for wanting to be wanted? – Sit, Eric, we're not leaving till I've finished this drink, if you walk out then we're lepers –

Eric Daisy said you'd do this.

Pause.

Ivar What?

Eric I want to go.

Ivar What did 'Daisy' say?
  I don't pay you to talk to my mother, actually.

Eric Yes you do – if I didn't who would?

Ivar Not about *me*. And by the way, the first-name terms, when did Mrs Elyot allow the help to / start –

Eric Help? –

Ivar What did she say? Bitch.

Eric You don't know anything about her.

Ivar I know she didn't want me.

Eric You've got that right.

Ivar is stung. Eric looks about, head low.

I never wanted to come in here, Ivar –

Ivar You didn't want to come in here with *me*. No more games, it's not a / *game* –

Eric He's looking –

Ivar I can't leave, I swear I'll make it worse for you if you try, I can't / do that –

Eric She said one day you'd go off, all right?
Why do you always push it? He's too much, she said. You have to leave him, he's, he's a bully like his father –

Ivar Like my father?

Eric – he's too fanatical, marching through Hyde Park sticking his finger up to the rest of us, he's too political, ramming it down / our throats –

Ivar How can you be *too* / *political*?

Eric – Leave him before he dies, if you stay he'll kill you, they're dropping like flies and it's their own doing, / Eric.

Ivar Yes, that does sound like her, 'dropping like flies', 'their own doing'. She said, *before I die*?
I'm not sick. (*To pub.*) I haven't got it, everyone. (*To Eric.*) And even if I did –

Eric You don't know me.

Ivar Actually, I / do.

Eric I don't want this –

Ivar sniggers, just like Robert.

Yeah, put me in my place again –

Ivar Do you know what you 'don't want'? Embarrassment. I wish I could say my mother was scared of me dying, but she's not, she's scared it's going to be unpleasant. These parents who can't find their grief at their own sons' funerals. Death by buggery! Scandal! Well, *I'm* scandalised: fuck my mother's fucking gentility –

Eric The landlord –

Ivar We'll go when I've finished – I'm sorry, but what she said to you, it's just . . . the *done thing* . . . and it's no way to live. It's the only thing I know about Daisy Elyot: Unpleasant Things terrify her, and I've always fought that, because without embarrassment you risk nothing and wipe out whole decades in a fog of gin –

Eric I asked you not to speak to that actress, I told you I wanted to go home. The way you talked about me, it's such crap. And it's *always* a game with you, Ivar: *I'm* your game. Every day, I'm your little project. (*Pushes money across table.*) This music, that play – I hated the *Doll's House*, I didn't understand a cocking word of / it –

Ivar Put that / away –

Eric No, I want to pay – and *The Swimming Pool Library*'s a shit book!

Ivar It really isn't – you can't afford this –

Eric I'm not your dress-up dolly bird, I've had enough of the *rich queen's finishing school*.

   Pause.

Ivar That's a pity. Tomorrow I thought we'd see the new Yugoslavian film at the Renoir.

Eric Oh, the new Yugoslavian film at the Renoir, I can't wait to not know what the fuck's happening.

Ivar Who cares, I just want to suck you off in the back row.

Eric See, you're funny, but you're not listening –

Ivar We both know what the problem is here. You just need to make being gay your ordinary life.

Eric No, you know sod all about real life. You run an art gallery and live in a flat in Holland Park that's all white except for the huge photo of the tiny flower with the huge whatsit –

Ivar Stamen, darling, it's a Mapplethorpe.

Eric It's a big pink hard-on!

Ivar See, she's a born queen.

Eric I just wanted to go to the gay pub down the road but oh no, we have to come in here and flaunt it –

Ivar I didn't feel like discussing Scandinavian heroines in a leather bar –

Eric But it's private there, you said we had that, you said that's where / we could –

Ivar I just meant it's a choice, I don't mean exclusively, we can't go popping Es and porking like slags in the cubicles in Heaven every night, and especially not when you're so deep in the closet / you're in Narnia –

Eric Maybe I'm not, maybe there's no closet for me to come out of: and I don't have to come out if I don't want to: *respect me, please.*

Ivar Respect yourself.

He takes a deliberately small sip: he's not moving. Long pause.

Eric You want me in your mum's face, don't you? You get off on the fact that every day the nurse who sucks your dick cleans her piss. Daisy is very . . . proper . . . and lonely . . . and she sort of *dies* with this love for you that's more hate than love, and I get it . . . because you never turn it off, ever. She's right: you're embarrassing.

Pause.

Ivar You know, you should actually read that tabloid you buy.

Eric And to top it all what really gets you hard is that you're slumming it.

Ivar No. I'm not falling for that class war bullshit, I'm not a snob, I'm gay, and you're the one who looks down on me for being *too* gay and I, I, I am very offended.

Because I'm right. Everything I said to that actress I believe: we're family. I know you're scared of losing yours but . . . do you know why according to them I can't be your swain? Because the law says no, it actually says we have '*pretended* family relationships' and I can't live with the deformed logic of that. What's an ideal family, scum like him? (*Landlord.*) Or the terrifying example of my mother and father? Schools are allowed to say people like Daisy and Robert are acceptable and actually prohibited from saying we are, because gay sex means moral Chernobyl – because heterosexual sex between Mr and Mrs Hindley of Yorkshire never results in Myra, does it?

Eric Jesus fucking Christ –

Ivar All right, I'm a bit much sometimes, but I'm not a hypocrite.

Fine, it's why I dragged us in here. You can't contain your queerness to some cummy corner of the Coleherne and be 'normal' everywhere else, Eric. You can't lie to yourself – that's what that play was about – if you don't say 'This is me' you're not free, you have to ram Section 28 up that lady's arse and blow it up like a North Sea rig, 'Pride', you bugger, it's a good word, so just admit you're wearing Paul Smith boxer shorts, explain to your mother the real reason Elton divorced Renate, and come out, out, *Maggie fucking out.*

I actually hate my mother sometimes. I tried. I knew there was something wrong with her when I was about nine. She took me to the Tate, it was so weird. There's this painting of the Lady of Shalott, it's Victorian vomit but I love it, she's about to drown, she's sobbing, my neurons were like erections, I think it was when I knew who I wanted to be – and Mother? Nothing. Stood there, carved in ice. You know the only time I saw her melt? Last year when Enoch Powell lost his seat. You could bludgeon a kitten she'd be stiff-upper-lip but Rivers-of-Blood Enoch's on BBC1 and it's tears for England. It's why I pass her off to people like you. To say what she said to you about me. To be so hurtful. If you think your child's about to die because the world wants to kill him, aren't you meant to grab him and hold him and not let go? She worships some cruel, intensely British god – it's not Aids that threatens me, it's good taste.

Eric, life is beautiful . . . (*À la* Cabaret's *Emcee.*) Ze orchestra is beaudiful, our time is now.

Eric What's so good about now?

Ivar Oh come on. (*Re. Landlord.*) There's always going to be one cockhead supremacist from the National Front in your face, you don't know how good we have it!

They manage a laugh. Silence.

Tell your mates. Tell your parents. Invite me for dinner on Friday, I swear I won't mention Liza Minnelli. Listen to me. The people who matter won't care.

Eric People do care. Your mother cares. *You* are why you lost your mother.

The cruelty of this isn't deliberate, and Ivar works hard to let it pass.

Ivar I don't want you to go back to her tomorrow. I'll support you till you find a new job.

Eric I have to help her with her lounge.

Ivar (*antagonised by it all, snaps*) My mother would never say lounge, darling.

Eric What?

Ivar It's sitting room.

Pause.

Eric I had a girlfriend when I met you. I don't need you.

Ivar I know – (*Empties glass: a gauntlet.*) Now fuck off back to Narnia.

Eric Daisy . . . Daisy's going to help me.

Ivar With what, the last bottle of Tanqueray under the bed?

Eric She doesn't look down on me –

Ivar I assure you, she . . . Oh, wait . . . wait, are you *her* little project? Is that what she's up to? A spot of aversion therapy? 'Leave the invert, Eric, go home to your gelfriend.' Lydia, that's her name, yeah? What's Mother offered to do, pay for the wedding? I'll find Lydia, your parents, your mates, *I'll* tell them. I'll tell them how we met – yeah, it was on the Heath, he had ten faggots up his trifle at once, very sordid, but then you see I was the stranger who *actually spoke to him* –

Eric I wish you never had –

Ivar My mother has it the wrong way round, I'm not putting *you* at risk, your self-hatred and anonymous fucks are going to kill *me* –

Eric I'm only twenty, Ivar, why is everything you say always right, I'm not always wrong, I'm only twenty!

He is very upset. They both are.

I'm scared. I feel hated and trapped . . .

Ivar Not by me –

Eric Yes by you, by everyone.

Ivar I'm sorry . . . Please don't leave me . . . I'm sorry . . .

Silence.

Eric Why was it weird your mum took you to the Tate? When she was an art teacher?

Ivar What? (*Hopeless laugh.*) You see? Lies. Envy. She can't even give me my job – art is my identity, mine. Why does she hate me? Why is she talking to you, what's she doing? I know she's lonely without my father but it's very rude of her to make my unhappiness her singular purpose in life.

Eric She's not lonely without your father, Ivar. Your father raped her.

Pause: Ivar is very shocked.

Ivar Just . . . stop this . . . don't be stupid . . . I was mad to let you near her, stay away from her . . .

A song – Bronski Beat's 'Smalltown Boy'. Eric begins to leave.

Don't go.

Eric Mrs Elyot has this way. She kissed me. We kissed.

Ivar Yeah, well she's straight like you so I suppose she's a better shag than I am.

Landlord approaches for the empty glass.

Landlord Bye, poofters.

Ivar Oh, they just put a gay song on your juke-box, you intolerable Nazi.

Eric has left him. What Eric said finally lands.

Eric? Eric?

The beat drops in and he is lost to the past. Eric becomes part of the transition. Wife's *Stage Managers/ Dressers help as he: kicks off his shoes, removes his trousers, puts on a female wig, headphones and a multi-coloured shawl. He dances, the music mashes with something new, and he is Cas, early twenties. Suzannah enters, in male clothes. Cas's dance becomes furious. Some moves suggest a flourishing tambourine, though there isn't one. A fringe theatre, gender-twisting staging.*

Suzannah You're crazy, Nora. Nora, stop it! Nora, stop!

Cas Look at me, look!

Suzannah But it's like you want to kill yourself.

Cas No, the opposite: I'm dancing to live, if I stop I'll die.

Suzannah Stop! I said stop! Nora, stop, that's / enough, stop –

Cas Stop stop stop please can we stop for one sec? Stop!

Music out, a disconcerting technical interruption: is it Wife? *Stage Manager deals with things. Character Actress enters on cue as Nursemaid carrying and calming a crying baby. Her moves are the same as before, and as before her costume is 1879 traditional – though she vapes.*

Character Actress Ms Helmer?

Cas I said stop?

Character Actress Sorry. (*To Suzannah, sotto.*) Isn't that my cue?

Director's Voice (*from the God-mike*) What is it, Cas?

Cas Does it feel organic, Suzannah coming round the front like that or does it kind of make my deconstructed tarantella a bit *too* deconstructed? (*Re. wig.*) And something's wrong, please can I just have three minutes?

Director's Voice Someone check Cas's wig please. One minute – we have to finish teching Act Two this session, peeps, let's keep it moving.

Stage Manager mutters into headset as Cas leaves. Character Actress swings the prop baby by the foot and she and Suzannah gossip downstage.

Suzannah My dream role: Nora. Hamlet for women. And I end up in a gender-fucked production in fucking Kilburn playing her motherfucking husband.

Projection

2019

Blackout, music – Pet Shop Boys, perhaps.

And interval.

Act Three

Clare and Finn, both late twenties, have just arrived at a corner table. It's not busy.

Finn All right?

Clare Nervous.

Finn Don't be.

Phone buzzes. Looks, shows her.

Clare Four hundred? Where's it all going to come from? We should just do it in Greenwich Park with your dog as best man and a bottle of tequila.

Finn I'd be cool with that.

Clare You'd be cool with anything.

Finn What shall I get?

Clare Um, he'll definitely drink. Red. No, white.

Finn It'll be OK, Clare.

He leaves. Her phone buzzes. Suzannah ambles in, wearing the same clothes – perhaps with added Jackie O sunglasses – drinking, hands-free on her phone. Clare recognises her, can't help eavesdropping.

Suzannah . . . No, the bar opposite, I can't go on tonight unless I'm drunk.

I didn't get out of my costume, it's a hassle after matinees.

Course I'm not wearing a frock-coat, as if we're doing it in period? – or Norway – I look like a drag-king coal miner, it's Kilburn, nobody batted an eyelid.

Oh, the most original thing a director could do is set it in Oslo in 1879 – you know, be radical, just do the fucking play.

How's my wife? He's still a prick. (*Glances about; who's here?*) And you know in real life he's the cheating *husband*; it's his other half who's the Stepford Wife, cooking him dinner while he's off shagging his way through Tinder and Grindr.

Oh, women, men, sheep – he shagged the old woman who does wigs.

Be single and child-free like me, then there are no lies.

Yeah, I know.

Yeah, I know.

Brexit. I miss 1997.

Yeah, I know there was Slobodan Milošević, but it was better.

She leaves, Clare watches. Finn returns with wine and three glasses.

Finn Should I get nuts?

Clare Did you see that woman? It was . . . doesn't matter.

Finn attempts a consoling touch. They wait. They scroll. A Man enters. Late fifties.

Man Clare?

Clare Yes. Hello.

Man Hi.

Clare Hi. Thanks for this. Um –

Man Thank *you*. I hope.

Clare What? Oh. Yes. This is my partner – Finn.

Finn Hey.

Man Hi. Business partner?

Clare No, um, he's a nurse, would you like some wine? It's white – Finn could get red?

Man No thanks, I don't drink.

Clare You don't? Really?

Finn A Diet Coke, or – ?

Man I don't drink artificial sweeteners either.

Finn Yeah, no, cool, they're bad. Water?

Man I'm fine, thanks. You got in OK? Everything all right?

Clare Yes. Perfect.

Pause.

Man So you see the kind of work I do.

Clare Yes.

Man It's intimate.

Finn Cosy.

Man The company's newish . . . my background's different, though not unrelated . . .
    So. As I said in my email . . .

Clare Yes, thanks for getting back to me . . .

Man Thanks for getting in touch.
    So as I said, as it happens I am looking for investors. I couldn't find that you'd done anything . . . so . . . Full disclosure . . . you know it's a notoriously risky business?

Clare I'm a doctor.

Man Yes, you said.

Clare I'm specialising in sexual health, so that will always keep me in work but won't make me rich – well, actually it could, stinking, but I'm passionate about the NHS so I don't have any spare money to invest in . . . anything, really.

Finn's phone buzzes, he looks.

I prefer honesty.

Man Fine. That's fine. No hard feelings.

Clare Um –

Man Clearly, you hated it. That's fine. As you say, honesty's / good, so –

Clare No, you don't get it, I liked it, sort of – I did wonder if maybe the / original –

Finn Oh man, wrong end of stick, we loved it, it was super-brilliant –

Clare It's just it's not why I'm here.
I misrepresented things . . . in my email, because . . .

Finn She's not a liar. She's famous for being honest, actually, like super-blunt?

Clare Are you sure you don't want a mineral / water?

Man What I want is investment, otherwise I don't want anything from you. No offence.

Finn Yeah, cool, none taken –

Man I arranged your tickets in good faith and / I –

Finn Absolutely, absolutely –

Clare I do have something to . . . not offer, maybe, I don't know, ask . . . don't go. Thank you for your good faith, I have something to propose.

Man But you're not interested in my company?

Clare No. Well, yes, because I'm fascinated by everything about you. That was weird.

Finn It's all right, Clare.

Pause.

Clare My parents divorced when I was five.

Pause.

Man Mine were unhappily married till my father wrapped his car round an oak tree.

Finn Oh man, sorry to hear that. Ice on the road, or . . .?

Man is 'WTF?' Pause.

Clare Dad emigrated to Australia . . . and once when I was a teenager I went to Adelaide for Christmas. It was so hot . . . this depressing suburb . . . Dad had an Aussie twang and said he was going to buy a vineyard. I thought, whatever, I was fifteen and moody, it was a crap holiday, and not even a koala park could compensate for the hate I felt towards my mother for making me go.

One night, Dad cooked me chow mein, drank beer . . . and he told me about the love of his life. This inspiring man, he said. I so didn't care because I'd worked hard when I was growing up to separate his being gay from his not-being-around, it was a big part of my identity. (*On one hand:*) Yeah, Dad's gay, you have a problem with that? (*The other:*) Um, Dad left us, big problem, lots of unresolved issues, right to be really angry . . . especially in that lonely place . . . with all the flies.

I forgot about the night with chow mein. A-Levels, Medicine, and it's so far away, he was hopeless at the time difference, and I just told myself: lots of people don't have dads, he left you, you don't need him, he's probably a psychopath or racist.

Finn laughs nervously.

Clare Six weeks ago he was shot. You know, that . . . incident . . . that rally in Melbourne? The gunman? Six people were murdered, he was one of them.

Eric. My father was Eric Hurst?

Anyway, I wanted you to know. I think maybe if he'd . . . wrapped his car round a tree . . . I might not have got in touch with you, but because it was a march . . .

Ivar. I'm sorry I arranged this under false pretences. I don't know anything about theatre, let alone investing in it. But I didn't want to freak you out, I wanted to make sure we could talk.

You're freaked out.

Finn She's really sorry –

Clare You see Eric – Dad – was going to come over for our wedding –

Finn We're getting married on the 24th –

Clare – and the thing is, I'm surprised by how sad I am he's not going to be here. The night after we heard, something unlocked in my head and the chow mein night flooded back to me . . . I saw his face again, I remembered it all, it overwhelmed me, honestly, and I realised that when Dad spoke about you – Ivar – I saw something alive in him, he was so alive. He said you were a firebrand – I remember that word because it was so pompous for him – and he also described you as queer, this was years ago when that still felt kind of militant, and that's why this is so important, Gay Liberation Front queer, he said – and it gave you this freedom, you kicked against everything, you were always in opposition, you, you stood up and, and . . . the way he died . . .

And the last time I saw him in the flesh I was a cow, I couldn't even be happy for him when he told me he'd been deeply in love, he said. And that he'd treated you badly, I think, and fucked it up. You were the first, he said. And we don't forget those.

Anyway, I wanted you to know. I wish I'd known him better. And I'd really love you to come to our wedding.

Finn Yeah man, you have to be there.

Ivar Me?

Clare It'd mean a lot.

Ivar I have no idea who you are.

Clare No, but I want you to.

Ivar I don't know anyone called Eric.

Pause.

Clare I don't have this wrong. My mum's name's Lydia? When I remembered Dad's story I asked her, and she said yeah, there was an Ivar, Proud Ivar Elyot, I mean there aren't any other Ivar Elyots with a 'y' on the whole internet, Ivar. She didn't like you – why would she if Dad loved you? – but she said he should have just been who he was and gone back to you, their marriage was a disaster, obviously he was a screw-up then and he hurt people, especially Mum, but then again I'm here – that's that compartmentalisation thing I do so I only judge him on the things he deserves to be judged on – and you should know that in Australia he, well, he never settled down with one man, but he had amazing friends, and he volunteered for everything and worked for an LGBT charity and he was open and proud and actually I'm a doctor because of him, I think the sexual health thing is definitely down to him, and the fact is he died for who he was, and I'm proud of that and I'm trying to understand exactly why it was so hard for him to be who he was when he was young / and –

Ivar You have the wrong person.

Cas enters.

Cas Ivar? (*To Clare and Finn.*) Hi. (*To Ivar.*) Hi, darling.

Ivar Cas . . .

They kiss.

69

This is . . . Clare, and, um . . .

Finn Finn.

Cas Cas – great to meet you.

Finn Oh, right . . . hey . . . from the . . . I didn't recognise you without the . . .

Cas Wig.

Finn Yeah.

Cas And breasts.

Finn Right.

Cas You saw the matinee?

Finn Yeah. Nice one.

Cas You liked it?

Finn Yeah, man, a lot, cool.

Cas So how much are you giving my wife to transfer us to the glittering West End?

Finn Wife?

Cas I'm joking – about the cash, not the wife.

Finn Cool . . .

Cas Here's our account number and sort code.

Finn laughs, nervous. Clare is still, silent.

It was great of you to get in touch.

Kisses Ivar, is all over him.

Finn Yeah. Um. Drink?

Cas Can't, I'm on again in an hour. Go on, Dutch courage – Ivar's saying, though he doesn't touch it – (*Toasts.*) Cum in your eye.

Finn Er, cheers . . . so . . . how long have you two –?

Cas Oh God, we're on like our crystal meth anniversary or something.

Finn Cool. I bet you had a big fat gay wedding on Mykonos that broke Instagram.

Cas What?

Finn Mykonos.

Cas Mykonos?

Finn The, um, Greek island?

Cas Because?

Finn It's –

Cas It was Lesbos and Lady Gaga officiated and sang *The Sound of Music.*

Finn What?

Cas It was Lanzarote.

Finn Right.

Cas It was some other stereotypical gay destination from 1989.

Finn I / don't –

Cas A 'gay' wedding, Finn, really? We're very past that, I think? And when I say 'wife' it's more a convenience or ironic reclaiming from patriarchal structures?

Finn Right, / yeah . . .

Cas It's just that there *still* isn't a word?

Finn Cool.

Cas Which is fine because contemporary sexual identity and gender are non-binary?

Finn Totally.

Cas That was like a major point in our *Dollhome*?

Finn I really got that, that was awesome. So . . . you're not married?

Cas Yes, we're married, we had a wedding, not a gay one just a Shoreditch one.

Finn (*pauses*) But you don't . . . identify as . . .?

Cas Holy shit, you're like really getting yourself into cisgender hetero-normative knots here and you don't actually need to? I'm super straightforward gay, it's just that I didn't have my wedding on a Canary Island with Liza Minnelli as my best person.

Finn No, yeah, I'm / totally –

Cas (*phone buzzes, looks*) Sick. (*To Finn.*) Fantastic eyes, by the way.

Finn What? (*To Clare, terrified.*) Um –

Cas You too, Clare. Fill me up. Not literally, Finn, I don't know where you've been and I don't think *you're* on PrEP. (*Sotto to Ivar.*) He's too easy! (*Slaps his own wrist.*)

Finn Yeah, no, what? Yeah, deffo, what?

Pours for Cas, and himself, drinks the glass.

Cas Does she talk? (*Phone buzzes, checks, screams.*) Get leukaemia! (*To them.*) Sorry: agent. So. Wife? Finn? Anyone?

Finn Clare. C-Clare's the one who wants to invest in plays.

No, she doesn't.

Cas Fab. What you saw was who we are. I've done loads of telly but theatre's more head-on I think, Wife tells this

72

story about *Queer as Folk*, it's like this ancient series, he says when it was on you'd seen all that stuff for years in plays and Hollinghurst novels, men rimming and fucking with cooking oil, it took years for even Channel 4 to pink up, thank God those days are gone but it's still theatre that's on the LGBTQIA front line / so – (*Phone buzzes, looks, laughs.*)

Finn Yeah, front line –

Cas – so we want to extend. And we're looking to take it to New York, aren't we, Ivar?

Ivar It's an idea.

Cas An 'idea'?

Ivar We are.

Cas Oh bless him, the Good Wife – (*Pants like a puppy.*) Speaking of puppies, we've just got one, so maladjusted, spewing all over the Liberty rugs, thank God Ivar's got time to talk to all those unemployed people in Victoria Park, he has to remember *their* name *and* their dog's.

Finn (*pauses*) I've got a dog. A pug. Called Phineas. (*Phone buzzes.*)

Cas My awful friends said maybe I should get a cockapoo before we get a baby – so rude – so, Clare – (*Phone buzzes.*) Sorry, builders, whole loft conversion, I'm getting my own improvisation room –

Finn (*to Clare, re. phone*) Caterer. Won't budge. (*To Cas.*) We're getting married.

Cas No way, *I* want to marry her – is anyone going to say anything?
    Oh. Oh I see . . . you didn't like it.
    Well . . . that's our aesthetic, so . . .
    Investors. So many are money-grabbing cunts – that's not sexist or lazy, that's actually the collective noun, a

cunt of investors – but Ivar's got integrity, because art is not about making money for us?

Shame, I'd so love to have you round, I feel a connection? But it's all good.

Why didn't you like it?

Clare You're producing the play – for your husband?

Cas Yay, it's alive – but I object to the 'h' word? And it's not a vanity project, if that's what you're inferring?

Finn No . . .

Ivar Implying.

Cas What?

Ivar Implying.

Cas What?

Ivar She's implying, you're inferring.

Cas Thanks, hon. Let's turn the lights off in dictionary corner?

Finn And she's not . . . implying . . .

Cas Though what would be wrong with a vanity project?

Finn Nothing –

Cas If it's a game-changer?

Finn Which it totally is –

Cas If everyone's super-talented?

Finn I loved your Nora, man.

Cas Thanks, Finn. (*Phone buzzes, looks.*) And if it says things?

Finn It totally says so much.

74

Cas I mean it's a relic now, Nora's like a bit of a cavewoman, it doesn't even pass the Bechdel Test, that's why I rewrote it, and I found a / director who –

Clare Why did you play her?

Cas Oooh, you can't shut her up now!

Clare Why did you play Nora?

Cas Well, as we say: if you have to ask. (*To Finn.*) To make a modern audience really relate to the outmoded oppression in the original, we sex-blinded it to open up questions for *everyone* / about –

Clare Outmoded oppression? Oh yay.

Pause.

Finn Clare, / um –

Clare Outmoded oppression, Finn.

Finn (*to Cas*) I get what you're saying, you have to shake / things up –

Clare No yay! Women couldn't possibly relate to *outmoded* oppression.

Pause.

Cas (*to Ivar*) Did you go to Waitrose?

Clare You know, I hadn't even heard of Nora till today, but while I was watching it, I had this strong feeling that you were being sort of arrogant with it, generalising it, so you missed something angrily, specifically female about it – because isn't it about a woman *oppressed* by men, by 'patriarchal structures' like, like well, marriage: that's what she frees herself / from –

Finn Cool, it's all thrown up debate, yeah? –

Cas Wow. You so didn't get what we did.

Finn And actually, Clare, what does 'specifically female' actually mean? –

Cas Is she saying *A Doll's House* can't be intersectional and gay? –

Finn No, / no –

Clare No, I'm not –

Cas – because that would be *extremely odd*.

Finn Who doesn't like a pow-wow?

Clare – it's just you seem like a very privileged person, so why did *you* play Nora?

Cas Why did *you* take this meeting?! You don't have to invest in it, but you can lie and say, 'I liked it.' For example, I like your hair. Isn't that nicer? This isn't Twitter where you can just say what you want.

Clare None of this is the point. (*To Ivar.*) *You're* the point and I'm really confused –

Cas (*to Ivar*) Are you even here?

Clare (*re. Ivar and Cas*) – this feels so . . . deeply, deeply . . . *traditional* –

Cas Don't wait up, I'm going to Heaven with the wig woman, leave something warm in the oven?

Clare Oh my God, you're the sheep-shagger!

Cas What?

Clare (*to Ivar*) Where are *you*? Who are *you*?

Finn Clare –

Cas Who actually are *you*, Germaine Greer – not a compliment.

Finn Clare, why don't we / um –

Clare No, Finn, you're just as bad, stop being so nice, why are you always all things to everyone, it's like you have no beliefs because you're too busy respecting everyone else's, but your tolerance is really close to not committing to anything. Here's a test: what if I told you that Ivar and Liberty Rugs here are fucking cannibals, by which I mean not just actual cannibals but cannibal-fuckers: would you be super-cool with that?

Cas Wow, you are a / supercilious –

Clare Shut up!

Cas Shut *up*, Sasha / Fierce –

Clare Are you *tolerant* of the moral standards of someone who takes a rifle from his father's farm and shoots my father through his chest?

Cas What?

Finn Listen, you've really been through it. This is hard for you and I'm trying, but it's a minefield, I don't know where to tread, I mean / shit, man –

Cas What's hard, what's so hard?

Finn Why don't you and Ivar just, you / know –

Cas Her and Ivar *what*?

Finn You need some space –

Clare I really don't, all the space you give me every day is making me feel very claustrophobic, what I need is for you to ring the caterer back and tell him it's forty-five pounds a head because it's slithers of salmon on little pancakes not the cure for herpes, I dare you to actually disrespect me, take away all the space and throw me in a tiny kennel like a dog.

Cas FYI of the two of you, he's definitely the dog, look at his puppy eyes.

Clare *Back off, cockapoo.*

Cas Hon, if I threaten you it's because your slightly out-of-date hipster here is working a really old-school metrosexual vibe, OK?

Clare (*to Ivar*) You're married, you're really married to *this*?

Cas (*to Finn*) You're actually going to marry Cersei Lannister? –

Ivar Cas –

Cas Fuck's sake, look at her, all moist on her Iron Throne.

Clare casually throws wine on him. Cas is shocked, then works it; Finn unravels.

Finn I'm only a man, *I'm just a straight white man.*
I'll be outside. I'll just go to Pret and I'll wait for you there, all right? I'll wait. I wish I'd met your dad, Clare, with all my heart. I'll always wait.

He leaves.

Clare I need to talk to Ivar.

Ivar Cas can stay.

Cas (*answers phone on Facetime*) Hi, look what Kylie Kardashian did to my actual hair with actual – (*Phone to bottle.*) Pinot Grigio. (*To Ivar.*) I'm really late now.

Clare For a sheep?

Cas *Why do you think I shag sheep?* An appointment to have my rectum shaved, what the actual, I'm meeting – (*Shows phone.*) Vidya my Alexander Technique woman if that's all right with you, Lindsay Lohan, fuck, fuck, Lena Fucking Headey fuck. (*To Ivar.*) I'm *so* offended. Can you iron that white shirt, thanks.

Ivar I'll wait up. See you at home. (*Kisses him.*)

Cas (*to Clare*) You need to come with a trigger warning.

He leaves. Pause.

Clare To be fair, he did ask why I didn't like it.

Ivar Sheep?

Clare That woman who played his husband, she was in here, I overheard her / talking –

Ivar Please tell me she wasn't still wearing her costume?

Clare She said he shagged around, she explicitly / said –

Ivar I'm not the person you're looking for, Clare.

Clare Then why are you still here?

Ivar I've never had more fun in my life.

Pause.

Clare I know you were the love of my father's life, Ivar. I can feel it. And he said – I can't remember – that you *raged*. Now look at you.

Ivar Goodbye.

Clare I'm sorry. But he is so . . . facile . . . vain . . . and, and you just let him, you just sit there and let him – by your example gay marriage / is –

Ivar Not 'gay marriage', just marriage –

Clare – by this terrifying example it's, it's *wedlock*. We're so quick to sneer at the past and so pleased with ourselves for evolving, but the world's always built out of little prison cells, isn't it?

Ivar He's right, you know: sometimes it's better not to say what you think.

Clare I can't be a hypocrite, I can't lie –

Ivar Golly, aren't you impeccable? You lied to meet me. We can never know the whole truth about each other, and we don't have the right to.

Clare This from the man producing that play? Doesn't it provoke us to think the complete opposite? Why are you doing it?

Ivar You know why.

Clare What can my dad have seen in you if, if . . . if you're *this*? Where's *Ivar*?

Ivar I love Cas. He's witty, he's vulnerable, he makes me laugh. You're grieving – but you're out of line. (*Makes to leave.*)

Clare She said he was cheating on you, she definitely / said –

Ivar Maybe she was talking about me?

Clare No, you're the Stepford Wife, / he's –

Ivar And what about you, by the way? Who's that teddy bear, beating you black and blue with kindness? See, I had no right to say that. Cas and I are happy. Maybe you and Finn are and I just can't see it. Happiness isn't the same for everyone.

Clare My father died.

Ivar And I'm sorry about that, but I don't remember him –

Clare I think you do, and he was better than . . . *Cas* –

Ivar Listen. This is me. I work hard, I walk the dog, I look after friends' kids, I do Cas's tax and commiserate with him when he loses out on another job so I sell my last Mapplethorpe to produce plays for him that get marked badly out of five by people I sort of know, and

I'm happy for my friends and their perfect profiles and I try not to be envious, and yes, I'm *married* – we couldn't marry when I was your age, we can now, it's nothing but good, it's changed everything, I don't have to justify myself to you. / Goodbye.

Clare Well, marriage suits *him*.

Ivar Who brought you up?

Clare Yeah, that's another thing Dad said about you: that you were a bit of a snob.
    Have you given up on yourself?
    You settled and now you're . . . handcuffed. You wouldn't have dreamt of this in the eighties.

Ivar Darling, I was always handcuffed in the eighties, I think it was called the Shaft –

Clare Did you vote to Leave?

Ivar Oh, come / on! –

Clare He's humping the old woman who does wigs, by the way.

Ivar Is that what she said! – bingo, the wig woman! – she's in her sixties, she's dykier than Gertrude Stein, she wants to bang Suzannah! I'm sorry about your dad. But you've dreamt-up some cheesy *Brokeback Mountain*-on-Thames in your head and that's not my fault.

Clare (*scrolls on phone*) He cooked chow mein and drank . . . and . . . this is him . . . he was reminded of you by a song . . . Kirsty MacColl?

Ivar Jesus Christ – some Hampstead Heath shag floated into his memory when he heard Kirsty MacColl? She's a Proustian madeleine for every fucking Dorothy in his fifties, line 'em up!

Clare Yes, yes, I'm liking this: *this* is who he said you were –

Ivar We called them fuck-buddies, they went by on a conveyor belt like in *The Generation Game* –

Clare No – this is actually an area I know well – a fuck-buddy's not some anonymous shag on the Heath you never see again, it's a regular fuck, so do you remember *this* regular / fuck?

Ivar Whatever you're looking for, I don't have it –

Clare Fine, go home and cook Husband's dinner, don't forget to iron his shirt and leave the light on. You know, I'm surprised I haven't met Cas before: in the clinic. These drugged-up Grindr guys making jokes about PrEP, I see them every day, Ivar – what's astounding to me is that anyone could think men like this represent progress.

Ivar Now you're really beginning to piss me off – that is homophobic –

Clare I'm absolutely not / homophobic –

Ivar You're sneering at my husband because he's liberated –

Clare I'm not, it's because he doesn't know what liberation is. He wouldn't know the fight for queerness if it slapped him in the facelift – he's not exactly oppressed, is he? – because of what *people like you and my dad did*. And because you indulge him, sorry, but you do. So he steals that play and hijacks Nora's pain –

Ivar That's / nonsense –

Clare What does he know about what you went through?

Ivar We don't know much about the generation just before us, it's always been like that and I don't care –

Clare Well I / care –

Ivar Yes, he's facile, but there's nothing there to anger me. Everything he believes is heartfelt and I won't have it scoffed at – and he hasn't stolen that play, he's read it in an interesting way: that it's *not* about the freedom of women but the impossibility of freedom in a bloody relationship whoever we are.

This has taken him somewhere he doesn't want to go.

It's really not my problem that when Finn proposed to you, you said yes. (*Heads off.*)

Clare I don't know where else to go. You can help me know who my dad was. Mum said . . . she said he worked as an odd-job man for your mother? Daisy? Ivar, he died because of who he was – some people still do, you know.

Ivar Don't you dare. Cas has no clue, and neither do you – none of you breezy young shits know anything about it and I'm fine with that because it was the Dark Ages, it's better forgotten, friends dropping like flies, and that Finchley / homophobe –

Clare I don't think you can call me breezy, and my life isn't exactly free of people dropping like flies, or Tories, I'm sure you're right that I'm rude but a) I know much more about gay men dying than you do, and b) I'm *not* / apathetic –

Ivar It's gone, and thank fuck, and the world is better.

Clare It *hasn't* gone and the world's *regressed* – look what happened to my father – *now* is the Middle Ages, and you *should* be angry. Your eye's off the ball, you sold-out middle-aged git. Even if he's outstandingly silly, at least Cas gets indignant about *something*.

You had an impact. I know you did because of my dad. He was just normal, he wasn't extraordinary or anything . . . but I know he had this deep moral conscience because he drove nine hours to Melbourne from Adelaide to be at Pride that day. With his best friend . . . this nice man called Shan . . . and I think you had something to do with the brilliant fact that that's where he'd got to in his life. I'm not judging, and homophobic is the last thing I am – it almost feels like that's what *you* are because by refusing to acknowledge me, by letting yourself be shackled like you have, they just don't strike me as queer acts like . . . like the one Dad made when . . . he covered Shan and took the bullet, Ivar. Don't you care that it happened? Are you in such a bubble, so comfortable and conventional now, that you didn't . . . recognise his name on your feeds? Aren't you shocked . . . or proud . . . or something?

I didn't ask him anything. I'd give my life to go back to that stupid koala park to talk to him . . . 'Tell me more about Ivar, the man you loved. What was it like then? Why did you mess it up so much? Where do I fit in, Dad?' . . . Tell me about my dad . . .

Pause. Ivar puts his hand on hers the way Suzannah did to Eric, and begins to walk off.

I thought you were out of the closet, not stuck inside one, Mrs Elyot.

Ivar stops. Turning point? Clare changes tactic.

Your mother drank, right?

Ivar I can't talk about this –

Clare She used to promise Dad money – and she did give him some things –

Ivar I said I / can't.

84

Clare (*gets her bag to get something out of it*) It was just a box of old tat – but there's something about something I found at / Mum's –

Ivar I loved him.

Clare stops, stares.

My mother destroyed us. Did he tell you that?

Clare What do you mean?

Pause.

Ivar Your father was right. I used to queer the pitch, and make people squirm. I loved it.

I'm married because . . . Cas wanted a wedding . . . all my friends kept asking 'When?' – especially my straight ones . . . It's the best thing to do for tax: how could *I* be happy with anything so bloody conformist, of course I'm not, and my unhappiness proves I haven't 'settled', Clare. So well done for exposing me. Fine, my husband defines me, and diminishes me – like your fiancé does you, by the way – happy? You've outed the unreconstructed gay. It was easier for me when the cause wasn't won. We got what we wanted and I think more than we need, and I'm lost. It's harder, it's harder to get up in the morning, all right? I just wanted someone to care for. But I'm not grateful that I can participate in the ancient rite of as-you-say shackling yourself to someone: I didn't want that and still don't, I'm not content that you and I are now so homogenised that we have the privilege of worshipping the Gods of Marriage, Henry the Fucking Eighth and Elizabeth Taylor, because I don't believe in that, I've never fucking believed in it, I'm the child of two people who *never ever* should've got (*married*). Jesus, this isn't Ibsen, it's fucking Strindberg.

What you don't realise is you've just told me I've turned into my mother . . . so I do have a new front to fight because I have to fucking fight (*that*) –

He chokes in agony, like Daisy.

I saw her the other day. I broke a teacup. It was my
mother on the floor. Daisy was always cleaning things up,
mostly herself, but she never quite managed it. She was
a chipped china teacup, lying there, waiting to cut you.
I used to think I knew why – that it was me. That she
hated me like my grandfather and father did. But that's
my narrative, not hers. I don't know hers. I've never
known.

Clare Was my dad good with her? Did she like him?
  I've got something for / you –

Ivar I have to go and tell Cas I'm not going to be building
him an improvisation room in the loft and that on
Monday he needs to cancel his acupuncture to come to
the divorce lawyers – so lovely to meet you, Clare, but
I'm off to get hammered on Mother's favourite gin. I'd
quite like to do that with the old sisterhood somewhere
off the map . . . the corner of a blacked-out leather
bar circa 1988 . . . the secret West End salon of some
breathtaking lesbian in the fifties . . . in nineteenth-century
Hyde Park with a Guardsman with a Prince Albert. But
those places have all gone. Hurrah, liberation.

Clare I'll have a gin.
  The advice is not to drink when you're pregnant, but
one won't hurt me.

  *Ivar finds himself laughing, but not because it's funny –
  he can't take this, really.*

Ivar Your dad was a beautiful soul. He was my swain.
He was closeted when I knew him, but he was very
young and it was harder then. He had a kind heart and
he didn't deserve to die – I have to wash my face.

Clare Get doubles.

86

*Ivar nods, though really he's trying to contain his grief,
and leaves. Clare waits. She takes the tambourine out
of her bag. Finn returns.*

Finn All right?

Clare He's in the loo. We're just . . . we're getting
somewhere, so . . . please, Finn.

Finn I passed him outside, Clare.

Clare No . . . he's at the bar.

Finn He told me he wants us to leave him alone now.

Clare No. I want *you* to leave me alone now. He's at the
bar, he's getting us a drink.

Finn Clare.

Clare Get him. Go and get him. Finn?

*She rushes out with her bag but not the tambourine.
Suzannah enters, 1879 costume. The machinery of*
Wife *is exposed. Finn picks up the tambourine and
looks at it. He is lost to the transition.*

Suzannah I don't believe that I'm nothing but a daughter
and a wife and a mother. I'm a human being, like you.
I've got to try to be one, anyway. You have your religion
and laws, but I have to find my own answers. A woman
doesn't have the right to borrow money in her father's
name to help her husband? Society says that's true, but
I don't think it is – so who's right, me or society? I have
to find out. I don't love you. You're not who I thought
you were. You had the loan shark's blackmail, and I
thought: *now the miracle*. I didn't think you'd give in, I
was certain you'd say, 'Do your worst, tell the world!' –
and that then you'd shout to the world, 'I did it, I'm to
blame!'

Peter emerges.

Peter No man can be expected to give up his honour, even for the woman he loves.

Suzannah A hundred thousand women have done it.

Peter You talk and think like a child.

Suzannah And you like a man I could never live with. When he returned my IOU and the threat was over, you made it all a secret again. Nora was your little doll again. I don't know you at all.

Character Actress enters as Nursemaid carrying and calming a crying baby.

Character Actress Mrs Helmer?

Suzannah Eight years with a stranger, three children with a stranger.

Peter What about *them*, what about Emmy and Bob and Ivar?

Suzannah If I'm to make sense of anything I have to stand on my own. I'm not your wife. I've no idea what's going to happen to me. But I'm free.

Act Four

Suzannah in her dressing room, packing belongings. Peter hovering.

Peter You know about the farewell party afterwards? Even Harelip Marjorie from hair is coming. (*Chuckles.*) Cruel joke. What's next for you?

Suzannah No next, Peter, I'm giving up.

Peter Well, I'm dashed. After a matinee like that? One of our best, old boy.

Suzannah Not saying much. Let's not sugar-coat it because it's ending.

Peter Can't help it, it's ending. One more. One last dance of the tarantula.

He dances, Nora-like. Embarrassing.

Every night you walk out on me up there and every night it destroys / my very –

The dressing-room (1950s) phone rings and Suzannah answers quickly.

Suzannah Yes?
Daisy?
(*Sighs.*) Fine, Giacomo, but she'll have to be quick. (*Hangs up.*)

Peter Daisy? Oh. *Daisy.*
Suzannah, I, I know things have been difficult in your personal life, and I want you to know / that –

Suzannah Peter?

Peter Yes?

Suzannah The tarantella's not the dance of the tarantula *itself*, it's the dance of the spider's victim, to expel the spider's poison.

Peter (*at length*) Right. Jolly good, old boy.

He retreats. Suzannah is momentarily remorseful, then packs. After a time, Daisy enters. She wears a theatre usher's uniform. She has a bag. Suzannah takes no notice.

Daisy Hello? . . .

Suzannah Come in, don't hover.

Daisy Sorry to disturb you on your break. You usually leave so quickly afterwards and this is my last chance / so –

Suzannah It's fine – (*Turns to her.*) Oh. It's *you*.

Daisy (*nervous laugh*) Hi again. It's, um, magical in here.

Takes the tambourine out of bag, gives it to her.

This is for you.

Projection
2042

Suzannah is taken aback.

Daisy This play. This play –

Suzannah No one came to this play.

Daisy I did, every night.

Suzannah I've seen you every night. The usher who comes for free: we're a hit.

Daisy As a woman, and a queer woman, this has been the / most –

Suzannah (*reads tambourine*) 'I love you, Suzannah. Isn't that enough? Daisy.'

Pause.

Daisy I know it sounds insane, but I didn't write that –

Suzannah How old are you?

Daisy Twenty-two.

Suzannah Drama school? Last of the breed at RADA?

Daisy Medicine. UCL. But I'm dropping out.

Suzannah What?

Daisy This was meant to be a casual job, but it's provoked / something –

Suzannah No no no. It's only a play. (*Returns tambourine.*) Thanks, but I never want to see a tambourine again. (*Back to packing.*) On your way out do me a favour, drop in on Peter's dressing room? He'll be in there, drying his tears. That's what actors are now – the ones reduced to plays. Poor old Pierrots – sad, irrelevant clowns.

Daisy I just wanted / to –

Suzannah You're smart, there's nothing here for you, you know that.

Daisy I –

Suzannah What are you regretting, that you didn't do Drama at school – or that you didn't speak up when they scrapped it? – Get over it, you're better than this, you're at UCL, you've got – (*Taps head: 'brains'.*)

Daisy I'm dropping out –

Suzannah No: no one came, no one cares –

Daisy Lots of / people –

Suzannah – people don't want to look in mirrors, they want to walk through them, so don't drop out of Medicine for *this*: bye-bye: don't deify me: sorry, but I'm a cunt.

Marjorie enters briskly. Everything about her is 1950s. She collects a wig.

Marjorie Apparently it can't make it through one last show.

Suzannah It's just a bit tangled, Marjorie, that's all.

Marjorie (*to Daisy*) You again! You're infatuated, you leech. Leave her alone! (*Hovers. To Suzannah.*) Are you going to the farewell party afterwards, dear? I shall, if you do. It's so odd, one makes a family and then, puff! gone! Peter says you're retiring. Can't be true. I do hope you and I . . . Well. You know where I am, dear.

Suzannah I do, Marjorie.

Marjorie (*to Daisy on exit*) In *All About Eve*, Bette Davis says people like you aren't people, they're mental defectives.

She exits. Suzannah laughs, relishing the savagery, then gives up on Daisy and shovels down her dinner. Daisy hovers awkwardly. She leaves. She returns.

Daisy (*re. tambourine*) I didn't write this. It's old. I didn't come to hero-worship you, this wasn't to thank you for you, it was to thank you for Nora.

Suzannah Look . . . Daisy . . . it's just not touching to me if you see your life reflected in the fjords – it doesn't feed my kids – (*Gestures, re. dressing room, theatre.*) Dead.

She eats, and lobs items of make-up – and props – in the bin. Daisy doesn't move.

Daisy I don't want to be an actor. I just can't be a doctor. My mum was a woman who walked, like Nora – she left my real father when she was pregnant with me because that was what she had to do in that moment: live by being herself. I understand her because of this. My stepdad expects me to be a doctor like Mum, but she went after her career, and him, and me, and got them all on her own terms: Nora shows us we have to do that, to know ourselves we have to dare to walk / and then –

Suzannah Oh fucking hell! I hate Nora! Fucking dizzy Norwegian troll! Fine, walk – little tip: there are Other People out there. What does she think, there's no abuse or plague or loneliness? She's not some rare bird who gets to fly above the wreckage. If you ask me, she slams the door, walks as far as Sweden, sees how much the ice caps have melted and realises it might be better to fucking drown at home with someone who loves you.

Daisy (*fit of giggles*) Sorry . . .

Suzannah (*stares; holds out a framed photo*) My wife, all right? Our twin boys. The day I started this job, she walked out on us. Because what *is* this job, she says, what does it mean in our world, it can't be meaningful. And she's right. So there: me. Medicine will put food on your table and mean something. Forget Nora.

Daisy I can't. It does have meaning – for *me*, I'll cherish your Nora forever – so obviously what you created is bigger than you.

Suzannah They're knocking this theatre down!

Daisy I know, I'm going to protest.

Suzannah (*head in hands, moans*) Oh God . . . I'm so old. Just . . . prove you're not a mental defective. (*Re. tambourine.*) If you didn't write that, who did?

Daisy I don't know. My father, my real father . . . he sent it to me when Mum died.

Suzannah You're actual baby Jesus, aren't you, down from heaven to punish me for being an inadequate person.

Daisy No – sorry – I didn't mean to – it's fine – this doesn't mean anything beyond the coincidence, that's what's so weird about it – it was in a cupboard, I'd forgotten about it, it was only after I saw your tarantella on my first day that I remembered it.
    And I just thought you should have it.
    See the little sketch of the woman with the flower in her hair?

Suzannah But who were they?

Daisy shrugs. Suzannah looks at the tambourine closely.

Are these more names?

Daisy Yeah, they've faded.

Suzannah takes a magnifying glass out of the bin.

You threw a prop in the bin – you need that tonight for when Nora asks Mrs Linde to sew her tarantella dress.

Suzannah 'Gabriela / Za –'

Daisy Gabriela Zapolska, the only one I've deciphered. Polish actress. Also novelist, playwright and naturalist.
    Finn – Finn's my real father, I call my stepdad Dad – Finn didn't really know if it even belonged to Mum. It just doesn't mean anything. I mean it didn't till I saw you. Please take it.

Suzannah (*pauses*) How did your mother die?

Daisy Stomach cancer, I was eleven.

Suzannah What was her name?

Daisy Clare.
    This is going to sound . . . but could I buy you a drink after the show? It's not dead, you made it live, and I have to thank you. You can't refuse an audience member's

thanks – especially if she's a mental defective – that's not reasonable behaviour.

Suzannah chuckles – she is warming to her – but the tambourine is preoccupying her.

Suzannah You know . . . there was another *Nora* called Suzannah. Ages ago, 1950s. Suzannah Heywood. I know this not because we share names and dead professions but because she was a dyke. At school, I used to collect historical dykes, I won a prize for an essay, and Suzannah Heywood was one of London's great ones.

Daisy Let's have her round for tequila.

Suzannah Oh, she'd love to suck the juice out of your lemon – Jesus fucking sorry.

Daisy laughs – and enjoys the power this gives her. A moment.

Say Gabriela Zapolska played Nora . . . Suzannah definitely did . . . you don't think . . . these faded names couldn't be Noras, could they? You don't know anything about this Daisy?

Daisy shakes head.

Suzannah Shame. Ask your father again?

Daisy We don't speak much. He moved to Auckland with his family when I was little. He couldn't handle how perfect my mum and stepdad were together. It's like . . . Finn and I can't talk because it'll hurt.

Suzannah (*pauses, presses tambourine into her hands*) Your stepdad's right. We need doctors. Good luck, Daisy.

She busies herself. Daisy stalls at the door.

Daisy So this Suzannah was queer?

Suzannah *The Well of Loneliness*? – Suzannah was the bucket. Old joke.

But she doesn't look up from packing.

Daisy The story's lost . . . but it doesn't have to be, does it?

It's the 1950s. The Dark Ages. And maybe at first Suzannah was – what's that old word? – closeted. And this Daisy who wrote the message has no time for that. Because Daisy's, um, a bit like my mum Clare – her own woman and a bit insensitive but for good reasons, Mum used to talk about gonorrhoea over breakfast, it was amazing, she was amazing, everyone was in awe of Dr Clare, both my dads loved her so much, that's why Dad puts all this pressure on me . . . and why Finn moved so far away . . .

Anyway . . . the only way this Daisy can make closet-case Suzannah be true to herself is to confront her with this. On stage, where Suzannah *has* to read it: 'Isn't it enough that I love you?' Fuck 1950, isn't that what this stupid play's about? – 'Some men want to control us so we must control ourselves' – because Daisy's like on-the-front-line-super-feminist-super-queer. Daisy's like Top Lesbian in your essay on historical dykes, so dykeishly *right* that Suzannah *does* wake up, walks straight out of the doll's house into Daisy's house and and and they're happy. And that's their story. They lived.

Pause.

Suzannah They were scandalously married by a sympathetic homosexual Church of England vicar.

Daisy They totally were! This is Daisy on her lesbian wedding day with a flower in her hair –

Suzannah They wore slacks to Katharine Hepburn films –

Daisy They read Sappho really loud on the bus and they had like kids and their names were, I dunno, um, Emmy and Bob and Ivar, like Nora's in the play –

Suzannah Emmy and Bob and Ivar –

Daisy And Daisy adored them and Emmy was straight and Bob was trans and Ivar was just boring traditional homo and they had like amazing Friday dinners with their extended family where the love was almost too much, and and and it's because of women like Daisy smashing the world to bits for the children she loved so so much that you and I are (*here*) –

She chokes with emotion.

Suzannah All right?

Daisy I have to go to Melbourne. My mum hardly knew her dad, he was shot, and . . . if she were alive we'd have been to his memorial, I haven't even done that, why? I have to go to Auckland to see Finn. You're wrong: my stepdad has to let me at least defer, I have to go.

Marjorie enters briskly with the repaired wig.

Marjorie All fixed, dear, less Bride of Frankenstein. (*To Daisy on exit.*) We've a nickname for you. Venereal Daisy. Because you're so difficult to get rid of.

She exits. Robert enters, searching.

Robert Daisy?

Suzannah doesn't see him. He and Daisy stare at each other. Daisy delivers these words directly to him.

Daisy I think you're wrong about Nora. I think she meets someone worthy of her in Act Four.

Suzannah So do I.

Robert Daisy?

He exits, still searching.

Suzannah You can't go back to work like that. (*Offers tissue.*)

Daisy Don't give up acting, Suzannah.

Suzannah (*stops, pauses*) My wife's an environmental lawyer. Every day she goes to work to prosecute the monsters, and I read some script, usually about an environmental lawyer going to work to prosecute the monsters. Her job matters, but . . . when I was a kid, the only place I felt safe was here. What I love about it is that Suzannah and Gabriela would recognise it. It doesn't really change, because nothing much *can* about the relationship between us, and them.

They both look at Wife's *audience. Daisy looks at the tambourine.*

Daisy What if you're right? You have to write your name on it and pass it to the next woman who plays Nora, it could be *really* old, what if it came from the first production?

Suzannah Then one of the names is Betty Hennings. You know, the first reading of *A Doll's House* in England was organised by a woman, Eleanor Marx, using a translation by a woman, Frances Lord. The first *production* was by men – a rewrite called *Breaking a Butterfly*. You can tell from that title what Victorian men thought of the Nora who left, so they just wrote one who came back.

Daisy Shitheads.

Robert returns, searching. Wife's *machinery is revealed: everything is removed.*

Robert Daisy?

Suzannah The farewell party's at the pub. The Frog and Trumpet. You'd be welcome.

She leaves. Robert swigs crossly at a hip-flask as a popular song from 1959 plays – Shirley Bassey's 'Kiss Me, Honey Honey, Kiss Me', perhaps – and Wife's *Stage Managers/Dressers help as Daisy undresses to a petticoat, takes a pretty lilac dress from the clothes*

rack, slips it on, arranges hair, puts on a wedding ring –
becomes, in a few swift moves, impeccably 1950s. She
picks up a glass of sherry, and she is at a garden party.

Robert There you are, I thought I'd lost you.

Daisy And I *you.*

Robert Don't walk away from me like that, Daisy.

Daisy But the roses are so pretty.

Robert How many have you had?

Daisy Robert, it's still my first, I've been nursing it for
nearly an hour.

Robert Your father's arrived.

Daisy Oh.

Robert Come with me, we need to be seen with him.

Daisy May I take a moment to ready myself?

Robert He's not an ogre, Daisy.

Daisy I need the lavatory.

Robert Two minutes. (*Re. her drink.*) And make your
first your last.

He leaves. Daisy tidies herself, her tendency. Suzannah
enters, very 1950s glamorous. She holds a gardenia.

Suzannah Have you met Enoch Powell?

Daisy Oh. No. Though he's why we were invited, I think.
My father advised him on something or other once.

Suzannah I've never heard of him.

Daisy I'm told Harold Macmillan's going to give him a
Cabinet position.

Suzannah Let's hope Harold knows what he's doing.

Daisy Yes. Excuse me. (*Walks, stops, turns.*) Do I know you?

Suzannah No.

Daisy I'm Daisy.

Suzannah Then I stole the wrong flower from the hostess's vase. Gardenia, isn't it?

Daisy Yes.

Suzannah I was cornered, she wouldn't stop talking, I have my period and it just screamed 'Pluck Me!'

Daisy (*splutters, spills sherry on her dress*) Oh gosh, my sherry, what a fool. It looks like I've –

Suzannah It does. (*Holds out hand.*) Suzannah.

Daisy Hello.

Suzannah It's a beautiful frock.

Daisy Thank you. I feel rather dowdy next to you.

Suzannah Don't be silly, it's lovely. Tell me about you.

Daisy Um. I've just got married. To Robert. He works for my father.

Suzannah Is he a good one?

Daisy A good one?

Suzannah Husband.

Daisy That's funny. As in, 'Is he a good shepherd's pie or novel'?

Suzannah Well? Give me your answer, do.

Daisy Fair to middling. He wouldn't suit everybody. (*Points.*) By the jasmine.

Suzannah I see. Well, I never want to meet *that*.

Daisy I beg your pardon? Oh. Fine! Then you never shall.

Pause.

Suzannah Is it children next?

Daisy What? Heavens.

Suzannah That's what usually happens.

Daisy Yes, but only if . . . well . . . only if . . .
I'd like a little girl or boy, of course. I adore children. I'm an art teacher. It's a bit rebellious, but I'm holding on to my job for dear life. Do you work?

Suzannah I'm an actress.

They stare.

Daisy We went to the Lake District for our honeymoon.

Suzannah How sick-making.

Daisy Coniston Water was awfully nice.

Suzannah Well, you didn't drown in it. Did you come across any Swallows or Amazons?

Daisy No!
I'm reading a book by Elizabeth Taylor now – the novelist, not the actress.

Suzannah Is it a good one?

Daisy Very. She somehow gets my life.
Would I have seen you in something?

Suzannah Deadly question.

Daisy I'm no good at small talk. Actually that's a lie, my father is a great enforcer of the done thing so I'm very practised / at –

Suzannah touches her cheek.

People are looking.

Suzannah Who?

Daisy Daddy. Enoch Powell can't take his eyes off us.

Suzannah What's his secret, I wonder? Would you like to come to tea or something stronger on Tuesday?

Daisy I work on Tuesdays.

Suzannah Oh. Goodbye.

Daisy I don't work on Friday afternoons.

Suzannah As long as I pin this on the right side of your head then it means you're free.

She pins the flower in Daisy's hair. Daisy looks about during this, laughs.

Daisy So are you acting in anything at the moment?

Suzannah I may get to say 'It's on your left, sir' in a film with Cary Grant.

Daisy Really! Will you ask him about Katharine Hepburn? Keep this a secret but I have a silly . . . crush on Katharine Hepburn.

Suzannah Don't we all, dear. There: a gardenia for Daisy. If we were men they could give us five years for this.

Daisy Oh. Quite. Lucky we're women.

Suzannah I've been asked to play Nora.

Daisy Nora?

Suzannah *A Doll's House.* Ibsen.

Daisy Oh. I know a thing or two about art. I'm fascinated by how emotional nineteenth-century art is, how it gives the lie to all that proper Victorian behaviour. We get the past wrong, I think. I'm rather good on the piano, I love Chopin, but plays? Ignorant. Is it a good one?

Suzannah Middling to perfect. You'll come and see it.

Daisy Will I? And will this . . . Nora change my life when I do?

Suzannah One lives in hope that Noras *can*.

Daisy Will she?

Suzannah I think so.

Daisy Will she!

Suzannah Yes.

Daisy Will she, Suzannah?

Robert enters. Suzannah immediately turns her head from him.

Robert Daisy.

Suzannah begins to leave. Daisy smiles after her, and her smile lights the world.

Daisy.

Blackout.

The End.

Appendix

The following is a translation of the Norwegian dialogue on pages 35–6 for rehearsal purposes. A non-Norwegian-speaking audience doesn't need a translation, as the important thing in the scene, the shift of power from husband to wife, should be conveyed visually.

Suzannah La meg gå! La meg gå, la meg gå! [*Let me go.*]

Peter Er det sant hva han skriver, Nora? En hyklerske, en løgnerske – en forbryterske? [*Is what he writes true? A hypocrite, a liar – a criminal?*]

Suzannah Jeg har elsket deg over alt i verdens rike. [*I've loved you more than anything in the world.*]

Peter Fy, fy! Ingen religion, ingen moral. Du blir altså fremdeles her i huset. Men børnene får du ikke lov til å oppdra. Forstår du nu hva du har gjort imot meg, Nora? Nora? Nora? [*Shame. No religion, no morality. You'll remain in my house. But you won't be allowed near the children. Do you understand what you've done to me?*]